FESTIVALS

Oliver Keens

FESTIVALS

A Music Lover's Guide to the Festivals You Need to Know

FRANCES
LINCOLN

Contents

Montreux Jazz Festival

There's a brilliant online project called 'Things That Are Called Jazz That Are Not Jazz'. It's a directory of things that have the word 'jazz' in their name, but have nothing to do with jazz music. For example, you can eat a Jazz apple, drive a Honda Jazz, or spray yourself with an Eau de Toilette called Jazz. We mention it, because the great Montreal Jazz Festival has become a borderline entry to the list.

MJF today is not a 'jazz festival'. Unless you count ZZ Top, Nick Cave, Tyler, The Creator or Alanis Morissette as jazz (the last is definitely not jazz, not even ironically). But while the festival – which descends annually on the Swiss town bordering Lake Geneva – has slowly diversified, to the point where Grimes or A$AP Rocky have played, it of course has jazz at its heart. Status Quo may have headlined twice, but any festival where Herbie Hancock has performed twenty-seven times (a Montreux record) has to score highly on the jazz-o-meter.

It's one of the world's longest-running festivals, starting back in 1967, when greats such as Nina Simone and Ella Fitzgerald gathered to play the Montreux Casino. This first home burned down in dramatic fashion during the 1971 festival, when a fan (unbelievably by modern standards) fired a flare gun at an impossibly

About the festival

Location • Montreux, Switzerland

Started • 1967

Status • Still running

Notable headliners • Miles Davis, Nina Simone, David Bowie, Lionel Richie

Famous for • The fire that inspired Deep Purple's 'Smoke on the Water'

Kindred spirits • Newport Jazz Festival, North Sea Jazz Festival, New Orleans Jazz & Heritage Festival, Montreal International Jazz Festival

flammable rattan ceiling. This event was immortalised by rock band Deep Purple in their chuggy anthem 'Smoke On The Water', which so flattered the people of Montreux for being indelibly linked to rock history that there even used to be a waterside sculpture in the song's honour.

Much of the festival's modern star power came from Quincy Jones, who co-directed the festival for a time in the 1990s, and used his colossal networking skills to bring in such greats as Miles Davis, who played there just three months before his death. According to Quincy, Montreux has always been 'the Rolls Royce of all festivals', but today MJF offers an even jazzier mode of transport – the M-Train, which runs between Montreal and Gstaad, and offers a trip soundtracked by three different jazz bands playing New Orleans style jazz. One can't say jazzier than that.

'Montreux has always been "the Rolls Royce of all festivals"'

From page 10, in order:
Opening night of the Montreux Jazz Festival, 1981
Montreux, on the shores of Lake Geneva
Festival-goers relax, 1980
Chaka Khan and Ray Charles at the 1991 festival

Isle of Wight Festival

The history of the Isle of Wight Festival is really a tale of two eras: the original late-60s incarnation and the modern revival, from 2002 onwards.

It began as a one-day event, headlined by Jefferson Airplane, who touched down on the Isle of Wight in 1968, their San Fran swagger creating a frenzy of excitement among the island's youth, who were excited to simply see real-life Americans, let alone real-life Americans who proffered forth icy rock classics like 'Somebody to Love'.

But that debut year is mostly overshadowed by the power of 1969's festival, which not only boasted Free, The Who, Joe Cocker and The Moody Blues, but also witnessed the incredible spectacle of Bob Dylan playing at Ryde, on the north-east of the tiny island. It's one of music's greatest bookings stories.

After an almost fatal motorcycle crash in 1966 disturbed his prime, Bob Dylan retreated from public gaze and moved to upstate New York, just a stone's throw from the site of the forthcoming Woodstock festival. Yet, contrary to the mass expectations of attendees, Dylan didn't appear. Instead, for his pivotal comeback show, he had been persuaded to come all the way to the Isle of Wight by a team of three, including a twenty-three-year-old music rookie who worked at small-scale

About the festival

Location • Isle of Wight, UK

Started • 1968

Status • Still running

Notable headliners • Bob Dylan, Miles Davis, David Bowie, The Who

Famous for • Becoming so big that it took Parliament to stop it happening again

Kindred spirits • Woodstock, Glastonbury, Monterey Pop Festival

From left, in order:
Marsha Hunt performs, 1969
Huge crowds at the 1969 festival
Hippies dancing
Bob Dylan and Robbie Robertson of The Band onstage, 1969
Tickets from the second Isle of Wight Festival
A couple kissing in the crowd

local printers, Solent Graphics. Dylan arrived in the UK, shorn of hair and carrying a briefcase off the plane to media questions about why he'd chosen the Isle of Wight. His main answer: he wanted to see the home of Alfred Lord Tennyson, inspired by a short film the young promoters had sent him highlighting the island's literary history. He also found time for a doubles tennis match with John Lennon, Ringo and George. Truly, the grass always appears to be greener on the other side.

If Dylan's re-emergence on the Isle of Wight was a coup, the 1970 festival was the coup de grace – not just for the island but for a generation of music fans.

Guinness World Records estimate that between 600,000 and 700,000 people attended. Some say this was the biggest crowd of people the world had ever seen. It was certainly more than five times the normal population of the entire island, and about three times the capacity of a modern Glastonbury.

Where the previous year had Dylan, 1970 had Jimi Hendrix as its lynchpin knock-out act. The Who were on the bill, and were on hand to augment the festival's struggling PA with their own hair-raisingly loud speakers. The Doors, Joan Baez, Joni Mitchell and Sly and the Family Stone also made the journey over the Solent to the festival.

A contingent of anarchists, Hells Angels and members of the UK branch of the White Panthers (yes, an actual thing in the late-60s) caused significant agitation for organisers. They wanted the perimeter fence pulled down in protest at what they saw as the excessive entry price of £3. They set up base on a neighbouring piece of land, dramatically named Devastation Hill, from which they and many others could watch for free, some seething in menace, others flying swastika flags and generally freaking most people out – including the police, who were forced to leave the festival to run its course for fear of being vastly outnumbered.

It's hard to imagine what the Nazi-allying Hells Angels made of Miles Davis's set. Jazz sage Richard Williams describes the performance as 'the biggest audience ever faced by a jazz musician, before or since'. Clad in bright red and in the midst of a full psychedelic reinvention of his sound, the intense, trance-like energy of it must surely be the most transcendent thing to have happened on the island. It's rightly been feted as one of the defining performances of his life, and exists forever in the form of concert film *Miles Electric: A Different Kind of Blue*.

After the storm created by the 1970's festival, a rarely successful Private Members Bill proposed by the island's MP managed to pass its way through the UK Parliament, restricting large-scale events on the Isle of Wight. Yet in 2002, the local council voted six to four to allow a new festival to take place. Initially named Rock Island, it started slowly as a one-dayer featuring Robert Plant and The Charlatans, but has since grown into a 60,000-capacity behemoth. The Rolling Stones, David Bowie, Foo Fighters, Coldplay, Neil Young, Paul McCartney and Bruce Springsteen have all headlined the tamer, safer and more family-friendly affair, which somehow continues the legendary legacy of drawing big names to the small island.

Isle of Wight
Festival of Music
saturday august 30th 1969

Isle of Wight
Festival of Music
sunday august 31st 1969

Woodstock

Woodstock happened so that it would never have to happen again. It's the biggest, best-known festival ever, and yet pretty much everything that could go wrong in the planning of a festival did – *and* it didn't make a dime.

Like Fuji Rocks, Woodstock is a festival attributed to the wrong place. It didn't take place in Woodstock, in the Catskill Mountains of northern New York State. It was only an aspiration that the festival – subtitled on its eventual poster as 'an Aquarian Exposition' – would occur in the upstate town. But when permits were refused, with tickets already on sale and with six weeks to go, co-organiser Michael Lang accepted a thirty-acre plot – blessed with a natural bowl shape – owned by farmer Max Yasgur in the town of Bethel.

The last-minute change set everything back and put schedules way behind. More toilets were hastily organised, while deals with food concessions such as Nathan's Famous hot dog company floundered so badly that, come the actual weekend, granola was essentially the only thing left for the hordes to consume. At one point, three days before the start of the festival, the foreman for the site confronted the organisers with a choice: either finish the fencing or finish the stage.

This was just one of many problems. Rain turned the site into a swamp and there was barely any shelter at all. People were spiked all over the place, and announcements over the PA about the dangers of various types

About the festival

Location • Bethel, New York, USA

Started • 1969

Status • Ended in 1969

Notable Headliners • Jimi Hendrix, Richie Havens, The Who, Joan Baez, Santana

Famous for • Galvanising a generation and showing that music can change the world

Kindred spirits • Isle of Wight Festival, Glastonbury, Altamont Free Concert, Monterey Pop Festival

From left, in order:
Three days of peace and music, Woodstock, 1969
Ticket and the brochure for ordering tickets for the now iconic festival
A music fan at Woodstock in his car covered in anti-war slogans for love and peace
Large crowds descend on Woodstock
Jimi Hendrix during his legendary closing performance
Sly and the Family Stone onstage
Woodstock crowds

of acid frankly scared the bejesus out of Woodstock's more timid hedonists. Everything smelled of hash and flesh, the latter caused by a lack of bathing opportunities – unless you wanted to get naked in the pond at the bottom of the hill, ironically owned by the only landowner in the area who didn't consent to the event. The state governor deployed almost 10,000 National Guard troops.

Probably the greatest single thing that went wrong, however, was when 50,000 people sailed through the unfinished gates two whole days before the festival actually started. It meant that, with no way to evict them, the organisers had little choice other than to declare Woodstock a free festival. From an expected crowd of 50,000, final estimates put the eventual total at around 450,000.

Woodstock's many calamities make for great stories, but they only form a small part of its cultural impact and overall legend. Because Woodstock was the most successful unsuccessful festival in history by a mile.

In stark contrast to the Altamont Free Concert – the Rolling Stones-organised event a few months later that ended in such appalling violence that it killed the 60s stone dead – Woodstock was blessed with such colossal good vibes that adversity barely seemed to register. As such, so many performances have passed into music folklore. There was the opening set from Richie Havens at 5pm on Friday, who strode onstage armed with a strapless acoustic guitar which he played with the intensity of machine gun fire. Then the counter-cultural sight of yogi spiritual leader Swami Satchidananda Saraswati giving an opening

invocation, deployed early to calm a then restless crowd. Santana's set on Saturday afternoon was a genuine miracle, given that the band's leader was given mescaline by the Grateful Dead's Jerry Garcia just before he went onstage; he took it thinking he wasn't performing for another ten hours, yet, as was typical for many acts that weekend, timings had gone out of the window. Creedence Clearwater Revival played at 3.30am, with band leader John Fogerty feeling cheated that they'd played to a field of people sleeping.

Recordings of performances by The Who and Sly and the Family Stone have rightly been venerated for decades, while Joe Cocker's Sunday afternoon set – anchored around the then relatively unknown Brit's performance of 'With a Little Help From My Friends' – dramatically prefaced a thunderstorm that stopped the show for hours. As The Band, Crosby, Stills, Nash & Young and the Paul Butterfield Blues Band played through Sunday night into Monday morning, the festival's closing act had still not played. Yet by 9am, with over half the crowd having left the bleak, churned-up site already, Jimi Hendrix and his ad-hoc band finally took to the stage. He played 'The Star-Spangled Banner' to a crowd ankle-deep in garbage and somehow it defined a generation.

Due to not having any correspondents at Woodstock, *The New York Times* ran an editorial mid-weekend titled 'Nightmare in the Catskills'. Among many gems are the lines: 'The dreams of marijuana and rock music that drew 300,000 fans and hippies to the Catskills had little more sanity than the impulses that drive the lemmings to march to their deaths in the sea.' History of course remembers Woodstock slightly more positively. By the end of the 60s, America's young had been through a period of upheaval, trauma and threat. Woodstock was a rare chance for that generation to see that humanity could be kinder and gentler than their war-wracked parents ever expected. One policeman is quoted as saying they had never seen 'so many people, in so small an area, act so peacefully'. And even if it had been an even bigger disaster, even if that stage had never been built as the builders warned, Woodstock would still have been a moment in history.

Glastonbury

Did Jesus really visit Glastonbury, as alluded to in William's Blake's 'Jerusalem'? And if he did, can he really claim to be the true lord of Glastonbury?

Located in Somerset, Glastonbury is a place steeped in absurd amounts of myth and legend. In ancient times the area was known as the Isle of Avalon, where King Arthur is believed to be buried and from whence his sword Excalibur was forged. Joseph of Arimathea, who was charged with the burial of Christ, is said to have brought the Holy Grail back to Glastonbury. Others believe Jesus indeed visited as a boy with Joseph, hence Blake's 'And did those feet in ancient time, Walk upon England's mountains green'. Yet despite an almost biblical pedigree, the area is STILL best known for one thing: the greatest festival in the world. And the bigger-than-Jesus figure at the heart of it all? Michael Eavis, cow farmer.

Eavis was born in Pilton, Somerset. Worthy Farm, where the festival sits annually (except in its famous 'fallow years' when it takes a break so the land can rejuvenate), was his childhood home. He inherited his father's farm when he was nineteen, but had no ambitions in music until he climbed the fence for the Bath Festival of Blues in 1969. There, exposed to Led Zeppelin and headliners Fleetwood Mac, he was inspired to create something similar.

The first festival on Eavis's farm was titled the Pilton Pop, Blues & Folk Festival and held in 1970. Entry cost £1 and, in exchange, a modest capacity of hippies were

About the festival

Location • Pilton, Somerset, UK

Started • 1970

Status • Still running

Notable headliners • Radiohead, Pulp, Beyoncé, Stormzy, Adele

Famous for • Being quite simply the finest festival ever

Kindred spirits • Isle of Wight Festival, Woodstock, Reading Festival, Boomtown

offered The Kinks, T.Rex and free milk all weekend. Some years later, the poster for the first festival was reprinted in the programme; around fourteen people thought it was a genuine forthcoming event and duly sent £1 to Pilton Farm for tickets. It's a delightfully modern British miracle that a dairy farmer with an iconic moustache-less beard became one of the most influential men in music – but since the start of the 1980s, when Eavis took full control of the festival, Glastonbury has slowly become the greatest name in festivals.

When the iconic main stage, known as the Pyramid stage (which doubles as a cow shed the rest of the year) was first used in 1970, the event had been a ferociously hippie event, but fast forward to 1980 and the long-haired, lets-hug-everyone idealism had been muted by the onset of Thatcherism. Glastonbury was now run as a fundraiser for the Campaign for Nuclear Disarmament (CND). Overhead, visitors might see a biplane carrying a banner reading 'HELP THE SOVIETS. SUPPORT CND' (always in block capitals; biplane messages can rarely afford to be subtle). Nowadays, Glastonbury has become so woven into the mainstream that it's easy to forget the rampantly political nature of its history, but the renegade spirit that Eavis engendered still manages to miraculously bleed through everything.

Take Eavis's heroic battles with his neighbours, aka the quiet, upstanding farmers and churchgoers of Pilton, many of whom are understandably horrified by the influx of people to the area every year. Things got so bad in the early 90s that a retired Christian woman named Ann Goode, who had moved to Pilton from the posh

enclave of Hampstead, erected a giant white crucifix uphill from the site, pointing directly at the Pyramid stage. It was a battle not of good vs evil, but of Goode vs Eavis.

Eavis also played a noble part in the aftermath of a horrific incident of violence in 1985, when members of Britain's nomadic traveller community were attacked by the police on their way to Stonehenge. The event, known as the Battle of the Beanfield, saw acts of heavy-handed and grotesque violence – akin to the treatment of striking miners months earlier. The bleeding, bruised and brutalised traveller families were given sanctuary and safety at Eavis's farm. Soon after, The Levellers, a quintessential old-school Glastonbury band, would play their song 'Battle of the Beanfield' to the largest-ever recorded audience at the Pyramid.

Glastonbury's proudly lawless aura gave it a major edge over the years. Even the introduction of rave music on the Glastonbury site was done in a rogue, off-kilter way, with sound systems set up by cheeky traders who would throw parties from Wednesday to Monday. But probably the most renegade aspect was its habitually loose barriers and seemingly endless ways in. If you were an aspiring teenage hipster in the 1990s, you were kind of a dork for actually buying a ticket. It's hard to think of many successful festivals with such rampant swirling folklore about its ability to be hacked. A hole in the fence, a cheeky ladder against the wall, or a security guard running a racket ... there were seemingly endless ways of getting in, and while crowds would swell dramatically, with estimated fence-jumpers peaking at a possible 100,000, the festival seemed to

gently tolerate the situation until the local council demanded the building of a 'super fence' in 2002.

What's so amusing is to compare this to the situation today. In recent years tickets have tended to go on sale at 9am on a Sunday morning. Yes, Sunday: traditionally the WORST possible time for any fun-oriented party person on the planet. Yet demand is so great that clubs and bars notice an annual slide in attendance the day before tickets go on sale. And tickets tend to sell out in minutes, requiring people to organise ruthlessly and hunt in packs – communicating in shared spreadsheets as they try to book for one another. Many will even go into the office on the Sunday morning, sparking up every computer they can to access the website, and calling from multiple phones to improve their odds.

Yet despite its departure from the benign lawlessness of the 80s and 90s, Glastonbury is still definitely, absolutely THE most fun festival in the world, bar none. It is the adult playground of champions. The site is so damn big and fun that there really is – cliché alert – something for everyone. It is one of the only festivals where senior citizens are amply catered for: mobility scooters gently ebb around the Avalon stage, which serves up nostalgic bands and fish and chips, and sometimes has a feeling not unlike a branch of Wetherspoons. In a completely different universe is Block9, a dystopic rave enclosure that has become the late-night heart of Glastonbury; away from the prying eyes of the BBC's enthusiastic-yet-rockist coverage, it has come to define the post-millennium heart of Glastonbury. Despite being only annual occurrences, Block9 and its anarchic and burlesque-themed predecessor Lost Vagueness both reshaped the musical landscape, the latter showing you could rock a tent at 4am with vintage rockabilly records, while the former – via its celebrated NYC Downlow venue – helped foist queer culture and a disco revival on Middle England.

More conventional stages such as The Other, The Park, West Holts and Silver Hayes all have their own energy but exist to host the upper orders of each year's bill, a line-up that is always expertly curated and able to please Glastonbury's wide demographic. But it's the weight of smaller, cuter, more specialist stages that makes the festival so unique: there's the new-band energy of the John Peel stage, or the Greenpeace Field, or the kaleidoscopic Glade Area. However, nothing makes Glastonbury as special as the Stone Circle sacred space – a giant hill from which to survey the sunrise over the sprawling site. Like a mini Stonehenge, the hill is home to around twenty megalithic stones, each around 2.5 metres high, set in an oval shape (and parodied by Banksy in 2007 with his own on-site 'Portaloohenge', made out of, well, you guessed it). It's the place where battered festival-goers spend the morning, slowly and steadily getting very, very high. But, drugs aside, it does bless the festival with an access to spirituality that very few experiences in modern life can offer.

You rarely see the Stone Circle on the BBC's coverage. Is it right that the national broadcaster, which began screening the festival in 1997, has turned the once-anarchic weekender into a national institution, like the Proms or the FA Cup Final? It's hard to say. Yes, it has led to 'Glasto' (as the posh call it) or 'Glaston-berry' (as visiting American acts call it) becoming safer, more mainstream and family friendly. But on the flip side, when someone plays a barnstorming show, the whole world joins in the applause. Among the many moments that have defined the festival's recent history are: last-minute substitute headliners Pulp closing their set with that summer's 'Common People'; Jay Z trolling all rock music by covering 'Wonderwall' as his first song; rapper Dave plucking a young, innocuous fan from the crowd who turned out to be a titan on the mic; Robbie Williams confirming pop's revival with a roadblock Pyramid stage set;

a nervous Radiohead bringing *OK Computer* to life; Orbital playing a legendary set (that led Eavis to set up a dedicated dance music stage); Beyoncé covering Kings of Leon and doing Destiny's Child classics; and Stormzy playing the biggest grime show ever.

And then there's the 'Oldie' slot, which sees a veteran performer given Sunday afternoon to steal the show. It's a tradition that began with a set from Johnny Cash in 1994 and would later bring American legends such as Isaac Hayes, Al Green, Dolly Parton, Lionel Richie, Kenny Rogers and Paul Simon to the aforementioned 'Glaston-berry'. But perhaps the sweetest oldie moment occurred in 2016, when Michael Eavis himself – aged eighty – sang 'My Way' on the Pyramid stage with Coldplay as his backing band. On a stage that has made memories for millions, who could begrudge the man responsible for it all one little moment in the spotlight?

From page 26, in order:
The view from the Park field at dusk
Hippies at the second Glastonbury Festival in 1971 celebrate the summer solstice with music and dancing
The Pyramid stage at Worthy Farm, 1971
Poster for the first festival
A sunny day at Glastonbury, 2019
Negotiating the mud, 2011
The sun sets behind the Pyramid stage, 2016
Revellers gather near the Stone Circle in the early hours, 2009

Roskilde

Nowadays, Mogens Sandfær is a bespectacled Dane in his mid-sixties, who works for the Technical University of Denmark. He worked at CERN for a time, and in fact created Denmark's first-ever web page after a chance meeting with internet Moses, Tim Berners-Lee. But what makes Mogens Sandfær seriously cool is his role – along with two others – in starting the wildest party in Scandinavia: Roskilde Festival.

Roskilde is a beast. What began as a pipe dream for some idealistic Danish students in 1971 has become home to some of the biggest names in music and around 130,000 fans from across Europe, all drawn to the perennially friendly vibe.

Established a year after the first Glastonbury, there are certainly some glaring similarities between the two fests. For instance, where Glastonbury has the iconic Pyramid stage, Roskilde has the Orange Scene (also known as Canopy Scene). The original orange canopy was actually a cast-off from a Rolling Stones tour. Roskilde paid £10,000 for it in 1978, with Bob Marley the first headliner to play under its splendid orangey glow, and the colour has rubbed off so much on the festival (not literally) that people describe the Roskilde experience as 'that orange feeling'.

A one-time capital of Denmark, the town of Roskilde has a long history, dating back to the Viking age. The list of its festival headliners goes back a few years, too. Late 1960s hipsters such as The Kinks, Status Quo and The Incredible String Band were

About the festival

Location • Roskilde, Denmark

Started • 1971

Status • Still running

Notable headliners • Foo Fighters, Muse, Nirvana, U2, Ray Charles

Famous for • Its annual Naked Run, of course!

Kindred spirits • Reading Festival, Bonnaroo, Way Out West

among Roskilde's first big names, before it fell into a Glastonbury-ish mix of rock, punk and alternative heavyweights over the 1980s and 90s. One thing is consistent about Roskilde, though: they love Bob Dylan. The touring addict's touring addict headlined in 1990, 1995, 1998, and again in 2001, AND AGAIN in 2006.

Another strange tradition at Roskilde has been an almost gladiatorial contest to snag the best camping spot on site. Known as *Væltning af hegnet* (the overturning of the fence), it sees festival-goers arrive in their thousands ahead of the gates opening, all primed and hungry to descend on the campsite. This eagerness used to spill over into an almost ritualised charging of the fence, complete with local media and photographers on hand to witness and report on the annual toppling, though in the last few years security seems to have finally quashed the tradition for good.

Another amazing aspect to Roskilde is its Naked Run. Bizarrely, the only bit of Denmark's festival scene to receive regular coverage in *The Sun* newspaper, the event began in 1999 and sees genuinely competitive men and women race around a roped-off course through the campsite, starkers save for a bit of day-glo paint and their racing numbers painted on their chests. Winners of this annual hippie Grand National receive a free ticket for the following year, and the respect of thousands of cheering festival-goers. And like the race itself, Roskilde is a rite of passage for most Danes that refuses to get old.

'One thing is consistent about Roskilde, though: they love Bob Dylan.'

From page 34, in order:
Crowds at the 2018 Roskilde Festival
Anderson .Paak onstage, 2018
The race to secure the prime camping spot
JpegMafia performs, 2019
The audience in front of the Orange stage

Reading Festival

Ironically, despite its superbly rocky reputation, the roots of Reading lie in something called the National Jazz Festival, which shifted nomadically around the UK before settling at a permanent base in Reading in 1971. By then, the titular word 'jazz' had become a major misnomer, daddio. Cream, Jeff Beck and Fleetwood Mac had all played before its move to Little John's Farm, an incongruously green space on the outskirts of Reading's concrete centre. As it continued into the 70s. The festival's links with rock hardened before ending the decade with an influx of newer, edgier punk bands such as The Jam and Sham 69. It pissed off some longhaired Status Quo fans, but whaddyagonnado?

This spirit of regeneration and renewal bleeds through the festival still. Fast forward to the late 2010s and Reading's familiar, guitar-crunching headliners began to feel the heat from the colossal stars of rap, hip hop and grime. Dedicated Readingists will point to acts such as De La Soul having played in 1991, Public Enemy in 1992 – or Ice Cube in 1994. But where it definitely had an affection for more rock-endorsed hip hop deities in the past, recent years' bookings, such as Kendrick Lamar, AJ Tracey, J Hus and Skepta, and Drake's iconic walk-on moment during Giggs' 2017 set have far better

About the festival

Location • Reading, UK

Started • 1971

Status • Still running

Notable headliners • Nirvana, Rage Against The Machine, The White Stripes, Kendrick Lamar

Famous for • Being a full-blooded rite of passage for young music lovers and its genuinely iconic yellow posters

Kindred spirits • Download, Glastonbury, Wireless, Summer Sonic

From left, in order:
Taking shelter from the rain, 1971
The distinctive yellow poster with the 2016 line-up
Entrance to Reading Festival, 1999
Crowd surfing, Reading, 2002
Gathering around a campfire, Leeds, 2010
Tom Morello of Rage Against The Machine, onstage in 2008

reflected the listening habits of its core demographics: late teenagers.

Reading Festival (and its companion festival, Leeds Festival which began in 1999 and sees the same line up play both sites over the same weekend) is a rite of passage for kids. Its timing, after Britain's annual exam results come out and before the start of school and university terms, makes it the perfect weekend for teenage kicks. It's a festival more often associated with teenage misfortune than anything else. Everyone has a slightly twisted and grotesque Reading story, from someone seeing someone crawl out of an overturned Portaloo to someone trying to set your guy ropes on fire for no particular reason.

Reading has had some truly amazing musical moments, baked into the collective musical memory bank: Nirvana's Kurt Cobain being wheeled onstage in a wheelchair in 1992, Rage Against The Machine coming on hooded and in Guantanamo-orange jumpsuits in 2008, Travis Scott hoovering up the crowd in 2018. But as much as the hella distinctive yellow posters tell a story about musical changes over the decades, its core commitment to young people is perhaps its greatest strength.

'... its core commitment to young people is perhaps its greatest strength.'

North Sea Jazz Festival

It's billed as the world's largest jazz festival. Busting open the idea that jazz belongs in small, stereotypically 'smoky' clubs, Rotterdam's North Sea Jazz Festival is an unashamedly large-scale affair. Purists may say that 'arena jazz' is not apt for the art form, but as mainstream exposure to the glory of jazz dwindles, it's a small mercy that so many Europeans still get to enjoy this annual blessing.

It began in 1976 in The Hague and, like Barcelona's Sónar festival, was the brainchild of a music journalist. Having made a fortune from magazine publishing, Paul Acket used his windfall to set up the festival as a way of giving the six stages (by 2020, that was fifteen stages) to the greats of American jazz, as well as the titans of Europe's thriving, and avant-garde, jazz scene. Miles Davis, Dizzy Gillespie, Count Basie and Sarah Vaughan played the inaugural North Sea Jazz Festival. Fast forward to recent years, however, past a venue switch in 2006 to the Rotterdam Ahoy centre, and NSJ has acquired a much less ruthlessly jazzy outlook. Today, rebranded as the NN North Sea Jazz Festival, and boasting the badge of being the biggest indoor festival in the world, it has broadened its scope somewhat and embraced pop and rock acts that sit nicely with its core jazz factor.

About the festival

Location • Rotterdam, Netherlands

Started • 1976

Status • Still running

Notable headliners • Herbie Hancock, Oscar Peterson, Miles Davis, Amy Winehouse

Famous for • Maximising the concept of the jazz club to its most expansive conclusion

Kindred spirits • Montreux Jazz Festival, Love Supreme Festival, Jazzablanca, New Orleans Jazz & Heritage Festival

Left:
Miles Davis and his Fusion Group perform at the North Sea Jazz Festival, 1991

WOMAD

Bless Peter Gabriel – experimental hit-maker, WOMAD founder and longtime bête noire of the proverbial 'haters'. Few musicians have had their follies mocked so painfully as the former Genesis man, who was even the thinly-veiled subject of a BBC comedy mockumentary called *The Life of Rock with Brian Pern*. Yet for all the mad ideas, strange touring concepts and outlandish costumes, there is one creation that exists and thrives to this day: the World of Music, Arts and Dance (WOMAD).

Today, 'world music' is a redundant term. Many would argue it was always a redundant term, needlessly segmenting non-Western acts from the mainstream. But it's important to acknowledge just how rare it was to hear Nigerian highlife, Tanzanian drumming troupes or political Zimbabwean funk in the UK, especially on a festival bill.

It took a man as comfortable with outlandishness as Gabriel to conceive of creating a whole festival, held in Somerset at a place usually used for agricultural trade shows, to play host to Burundi drummers. 'Farmers were worried about the impact on the milk yield and of over arousing their bulls,' claimed Gabriel, years later. 'This was a time when I was being told many of my ideas were crazy, so I deliberately started incorporating synonyms for crazy into the names of the projects I was working on, so a synthesiser company was called Syco and this festival project became (WO)MAD – the World of Music, Arts and Dance.'

About the festival

Location • Wiltshire, UK; plus Australia, New Zealand, UAE, Spain, Italy, Chile

Started • 1982

Status • Still running

Notable headliners • Salif Keita, Baaba Maal, Gilberto Gil, The Drummers of Burundi

Famous for • Its devotion to world music

Kindred spirits • Glastonbury, Rainforest World Music Festival, Oslo World

From left, in order:
A dancer performing from a heliosphere balloon in the air above the crowds, 2007
Festival flags, 2010
Crowds enjoy the music
WOMAD at Charlton Park Mansion House in Malmesbury, Wiltshire, 2010

Gabriel and a loose grouping of journalists, artists and promoters who all shared a love of world music birthed WOMAD in 1982, having taken two years to raise the funds. Proceeds from the event went to UNICEF. Simple Minds, Echo and the Bunnymen and Robert Fripp all played under a huge, domed semi-circular stage. The poster advertised 'record breaking attempts, fairground and picnic facilities'.

But ambition got the better of them. 'We learned later that it usually takes three years to build up a festival: the first year is ready, the second year is steady and the third year is go. We unfortunately did our go bit in year one, and came a cropper.' The scale of the losses involved Gabriel taking loans just to pay the acts' wages. Eventually, his ex-Genesis bandmates did him a major solid: agreeing to a one-off benefit reunion to cover his debts.

So, after its miraculous, unexpected birth, WOMAD endured. By taking a huge gamble on world music, it did what all great festivals do – it created and fostered its own audience. Today it is a gentle, tipi-strewn, lentil-scented, family-friendly experience that enjoys such a glowing word-of-mouth buzz that it barely needs to advertise or market itself. Food, craft and intimate musical discoveries are its much-loved hallmarks. After so much struggle and strife to get it off the ground, the most contentious thing that occurs at WOMAD today is a drum circle keeping an ageing punter awake at night.

'By taking a huge gamble on world music, it did what all great festivals do — it created and fostered its own audience.'

Rock am Ring

Festivals make use of some pretty unlikely sites: farms, ski resorts, children's adventure parks, horse racing tracks ... but surely one of the oddest is Rock am Ring's takeover of famed motor-racing circuit, Nürburgring.

This legendarily treacherous track decided to get into the equally treacherous business of hosting a music festival for the first time in 1985. The 'ring' has been its most regular home ever since (over the years it has varied between a few sites, and also spawned a simultaneous clone, Rock im Park, which takes place in Nuremberg).

The festival-goers really do take over the track. The gleaming aluminium sterility of the pit lane, for example, acts as a gateway to the main site. It's a surreal meeting of two worlds: the buttoned-up world of motor racing and the beer-sloshing, fist-pumping, ready-to-mosh rock fans. Luckily, both tribes share a penchant for THINGS THAT ARE VERY, VERY LOUD.

Contemporary rock and metal are the speciality at Rock am Ring. Legacy rockers get a look-in, of course (Iron Maiden, Guns N' Roses, Rage Against The Machine and Rammstein are some of the perennial visitors to Nürburgring), but it has a great reputation for bringing up new talent, too. As with most rock-focused festivals, there's always been a small incongruity between the festival's aura and its actual vibe. Images of a ferocious mosh pit or a give-no-fucks crowd surfer in a wheelchair often betray the fact that Rock am Ring crowds are generally laid back and friendly as hell.

About the festival

Location • Nürburg, Germany

Started • 1985

Status • Still running

Notable headliners • Depeche Mode, Simple Minds, Van Halen, Iron Maiden

Famous for • Taking over a motor-racing track and making it even noisier

Kindred spirits • Download, Hellfest, Wacken, Sonisphere, Rock in Rio

It's also worth remembering that it's the only festival with its own branch of Lidl on site. With its strangely reassuring slogan ('You rock, we care'), this vast marquee space sells turkey breast and chicken schnitzel for people to cook on grills. See, we told you it was incongruous.

'It's a surreal meeting of two worlds: the buttoned-up world of motor racing and the beer-sloshing, fist-pumping, ready-to-mosh rock fans.'

From page 48, in order:
A sea of people at Nürburg, 2009
Ticket for the 1996 festival
Festival-goers relax, Rock am Ring 2019
The crowd in front of the main stage, 2014

Rock in Rio

For most people, festivals play a part in getting away from the outside world. Rarely do they have a hand in actually changing the outside world. Brazil's first Rock in Rio occurred in 1985, around a month before elections that saw the Democratic Alliance sweep to power and signal the end of the country's twenty-one-year military dictatorship. In part, credit has to be given to the nightly TV broadcasts that showed a bold, brilliant Brazil playing host to some of the biggest bands in the world over nine days: Queen, AC/DC, Whitesnake and Ozzy Osbourne were just a few of the acts on the heaving bill. The sheer ambitious scale of the festival proved a blessing for Brazil's youth, who had never experienced life without the constraints of the regime; Rock in Rio screamed freedom, as much as its hard rockin' headliners, well, screamed.

As a spectacle, Rock in Rio was definitely trying very, very hard. It was so vast, it created its own city, known as the City of Rock. It survives today, but the city itself isn't always Rio any more. Rock in Rio has become a movable feast: since 1985, the festival has hopped around the globe – in part, a reflection of how challenging it is to stage a festival in Brazil. To date, it has taken place in Las Vegas, Santiago, Madrid and, most illustriously, Lisbon. Nowadays, Rock in Rio annually alternates between Rio and Lisbon.

As the great Dan Stubbs from *NME* surmised: 'Rock In Rio exists in a unique space somewhere between a festival, a theme park and a religious cult.' This last might be a reference to the fact that the finale of each night at Rock in Rio is accompanied by the festival's own anthem. Other quirks of the Lisbon edition include the ability to ride a zip wire over the main stage – while the acts are playing – plus a swimming pool located right next to a stage. It's an innovation we'd like to see rolled out to every single sunny festival ever. Thank you.

About the festival

Location • Rio de Janeiro, Brazil; Madrid, Spain; Las Vegas, USA; Santiago, Chile

Started • 1985

Status • Still running

Notable headliners • Queen, Iron Maiden, Beyoncé, Metallica

Famous for • Exporting Brazilian spectacle to the rest of the world

Kindred spirits • Rock am Ring, Rock Werchter, Download, Monsters of Rock, Sonisphere

Left:
Freddie Mercury performing with Queen, 1985

Burning Man

No other festival in the world polarises opinion quite as sharply as Burning Man. Among the festival-going population of the world, it's Burners vs The Rest of the World: an epic battle between those who have undergone the mammoth mission of being subsistent and fabulous in the Nevada desert and hail it as a way of life akin to a religion, versus those who take one look at a man in steampunk goggles and dusty leggings and say 'no'. There is zero middle ground here.

The roots of this expansive and decadent feat of strength lie in a bonfire ritual on San Francisco's Baker Beach. Some friends gathered on the summer solstice in 1986, with a crudely constructed but still impressive eight-foot wooden effigy. By 1987 it had grown to fifteen feet, and by 1988 the structure was up to thirty feet. It was the start of a wild exponential growth that wouldn't stop until it became a week-long party for 70,000 people.

By 1990, word-of-mouth buzz and an inability to get a permit to burn the titular effigy saw the gathering merge with something called Zone #4 – a space run by the San Franciscan branch of a group called the Cacophony Society, which was described as a 'Dadaist temporary autonomous zone'. This was located in the Black Rock Desert, around 100 miles from Reno in Nevada. Black Rock City was born.

The festival site, known as the playa, is ordered in a grid formation based on coordinates that relate to points on a clock

About the festival

Location • Black Rock Desert, Pershing County, Nevada, USA

Started • 1986

Status • Still running

Notable headliners • Burning Man doesn't really do headliners

Famous for • Total hedonism with a rugged twist

Kindred spirits • AfrikaBurn, Nowhere, Midburn

From left, in order:
An art installation shoots flames in the desert, 2014
A tall sailing ship vehicle, 2016
Revellers on bikes and in customised cars, 2015
A sunset gathering, 2014
The ephemeral city in the heart of Nevada's Black Rock Desert, 2019
An art installation from 2011

face. Across this intermingled seven-square-mile space, cars are only allowed if they're 'mutant vehicles' – intricately modified, jaw-dropping shapes, festooned and often able to carry DJs and sound systems. Bikes are a much more prevalent form of transport, though, and allow visitors to traverse the playa; interestingly, this is never situated on the same bit of desert each time, though the lack of any natural geographic landmarks make this shift almost imperceptible.

Unlike every other festival in this book, BM doesn't have a centrally organised line-up or bill. All entertainment, apart from the raw infrastructure of the festival itself, is stuff that has come via the efforts of its attendees. It's the starkest example of the ten codified, written-down edicts by which Burning Man operates, as expressed by one of the founders Larry Harvey in 2004, and to which, remarkably, Burners still adhere today. One of these is centred on gifting, whereby almost nothing at BM has a cash value. Harvey expressed it best by saying in 2014: 'Burning Man is like a big family picnic... Would you sell things to one another at a family picnic? No, you'd share things.' Thus, just as there are no money transactions between Burners all week, so the provision of music and activities is part of the same 'gift economy' too. In practice, of course, BM's cache brings out the stars. Electronic music has slowly become a staple, with certain camps pulling in such big-name EDM and techno players as Carl Cox, Diplo, Flume and Paul Oakenfold. But this increasing mainstreaming of the event isn't without controversy.

Burning Man's culture of gifting exists as an exemplary challenge to the orthodoxies of capitalism, a way of showing that humans can exist – even just for a week – without the spectre of wealth. But in recent years, the event has drawn heat for so-called 'plug and play' camps that serve a rich, often tech-related crowd of Silicon Valley types, aided by the recent-ish construction of a landing strip for private jets. One camp named 'Humano the Tribe' offered accommodation costing $100,000, including two bedrooms and 'super-powerful air conditioning'. Humano has since been uninvited by Burning Man CEO Marian Goodell, yet it's still problematic that BM has a CEO at all, a job rumoured to pay $267,000 a year.

Certainly Burning Man is an economic success. It's got to the point of being oversubscribed, with tickets tending to sell out within an hour of them going on sale. And it's important to note that this money does go back into funding the incredible and unabashedly ambitious art structures that make the festival so utterly distinctive and thrilling to be a part of – the burning man itself remains a focus of the whole event. But despite the creeping influence of commercialisation, it is still a genuine miracle of ethos over economics. No other festival engenders such identity with its crowd: Burners are Burners all year round, proud to display it on their LinkedIns and dating profiles alike. People are indelibly changed after visiting Black Rock City and find friendships that really endure – whether that's in the furtively hallowed Orgy Dome or just getting a pancake. Haters will always hate, but the loyal devotees of Burning Man carry the flame regardless.

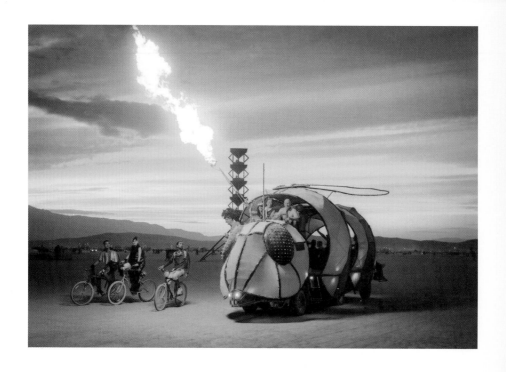

Love Parade

Germany's wildly influential Love Parade sat on a hazy borderline between carnival, free party and festival. Like London's Notting Hill Carnival, it was a completely free event and truly carnivalesque to boot, with Berlin's streets and parks filled with sound and floats. There's also a beautiful link between the importance of the sounds of both events to both countries. Just as bass music and sound-system culture, as evangelised at NHC, has come to influence every forward-thinking British sonic innovation (garage, grime, drum & bass, dubstep, to name a few), so Love Parade cemented the place of techno in the national consciousness of Germany. The enormous passion for electronic music in Germany, kickstarted by Kraftwerk and others in the 70s, found an annual place of worship – first on the long, elegant Kurfürstendamm boulevard from 1989 until 1996, and then within the enormous Tiergarten park, with the Siegessäule Victory Column and the bronze statue atop it becoming iconic symbols of the party.

The problem was that Love Parade became a pilgrimage for techno lovers from all corners of the world, leading to a dark tragedy years later. Back when it began, it was a tiny, politically minded demonstration attended by 150 people, which came with the slogan '*Friede, Freude, Eierkuchen*' – peace, joy, pancakes – though the latter was to highlight the need for fair food distribution, not simply a celebration of sweet fluffy discs, delicious though they are.

About the festival

Location • Various cities across Germany

Started • 1989

Status • Ended in 2010

Notable headliners • Westbam, Paul van Dyk, Sven Väth

Famous for • Being completely synonymous with techno music

Kindred spirits • Lake Parade, Vision Parade, Generation Move, Union Move, Reincarnation

From left, in order:
Thousands of techno fans on Berlin's Unter den Linden avenue, 2003
Partying in front of the Brandenburg Gate
Crowds gather around the Siegessäule Victory Column, 2003
The world's biggest techno party, 2006

'Love Parade cemented the place of techno in the national consciousness of Germany.'

But Love Parade soon became something truly irresistible: a free party boasting some of the world's finest house, techno and trance DJs. Just some of the names to grace the decks include DJ Tiesto, Carl Cox, Paul van Dyk, Sven Väth, DJ Hell, Armin van Buuren, and German techno monarch Westbam, who played at every single one and even composed many of the annual 'anthems' written for the event. A cacophony of whistles and cheers greeted all the DJs, who passed slowly through the crowds on trucks bearing water-cooled sound systems, each loaded with so much bass presence that Berlin Zoo claimed that 2001's event gave a substantial number of its animals diarrhoea. As the late-evening curfew began to approach, and with daylight fading, something known as 'Abschlusskundgebung' would occur – which eventually saw all forty sound systems join up and link to just one set of turntables. This was how a very small but blessed group of DJs had the bum-rumblingly frightening task of DJing for over a million people at once. No pressure, then.

As much of a draw as the music was the overwhelming freedom of Love Parade. It created an explosion of energy and abandon, which, for me, is what tips the German street party into the realm of being a festival.

While drugs and nudity are synonymous with the legend of Love Parade, there was a deeper purpose to it all beyond just hedonism. As author and regular Love Parader Wolfgang Sterneck said years later: 'At one point, I wished that the "acid sound" pumping straight out of the speakers at a Love Parade party would flow through the streets every day. An endless rhythmic beat, instead of the urban barrage of noise that otherwise surrounds us.'

Sadly, the utopian dream ended appallingly in 2010, when a crush of people entering the festival at its new location in the Ruhr Valley led to the deaths of twenty-one people, with hundreds more injured. Given the huge crowds and widespread drug use at previous parades, many commentators wondered how something similar hadn't happened before. Organiser Rainer Schaller vowed immediately that Love Parade would never return, making for a tragic and decisive end to one of the 90s most defining events.

Lollapalooza

Lollapalooza (n), an extraordinary or unusual thing, person, or event. Or a piece of hard candy attached to a stick, i.e. a lollipop.

Nowadays, it's common to see the suffix '-palooza' added to any number of events. A birthday party for Brian becomes 'Brian-a-palooza'. A discount sale at a shoe shop is 'shoe-a-palooza'. But it's possible this ninety-plus-year-old word would have dwindled into folksy obscurity had 90s rock god Perry Farrell not seen an episode of *The Three Stooges* in the early 1990s. It chimed with him at a time when his band Jane's Addiction were contemplating a farewell tour. A visit to England's Reading Festival acted as the spark to bring all these elements together: 'Let's bring Reading to America,' thought drummer Marc Geiger, and so they built the tour into a journeying festival. A journeying festival with a daft, ancient name, that changed the world in some profound ways.

Farrell's vision was a travelling charabanc of alternative youth culture. Rap, grunge and formative dance music were all exploding in their respective scenes, and Lollapalooza aimed to harness and amplify them. It was intended as a collaboration, 'a multicultural jam session,' as Speech from Arrested Development referred to it. It's first outing, in 1991, was certainly diverse for the times: Jane's Addiction, Nine Inch Nails and Butthole Surfers crossed the country with Brit-goth icons Siouxsie and the Banshees and rapper Ice-T. 'Lollapalooza was a little ramshackle errand,' stated tour

About the festival

Location • Chicago, USA (previously several other North American cities)

Started • 1991

Status • Still running

Notable headliners • Nine Inch Nails, Jane's Addiction, Smashing Pumpkins

Famous for • Being the coolest way to piss off your parents in the 90s

Kindred spirits • Reading Festival, Big Day Out, South by Southwest, Woodstock

'It was intended as a collaboration, "a multicultural jam session ..."'

manager Michael 'Curly' Jobson. 'The fact that it wasn't a slick, overproduced event gave it that element of cool.'

A sense of early 90s cool really did pour out of Lollapalooza at the start. At every show, hundreds of kids left with a f-u-mom-and-dad piercing. You could buy any number of hemp-based goods and pointy druid hats – Farrell once recalled that an on-site bookseller sold snuff movies and books about bomb-making – or, vastly more futuristically, try 'The Cyberpit', a booth of networked Macintosh computers that allowed festival-goers to talk with each other, find information and enter messages that would display over the main stage.

But perhaps Lollapalooza's greatest impact was to expose Middle America to the joys of stage-diving and moshing. Born in punk clubs and hardcore venues, they went national when Lollapalooza's audiences moshed in the beloved national parks and sports arenas of George Bush Snr's America. It was so new and perplexing to staff in each city that, as Jobson pointed out, 'We were having to educate security guys to not smash kids' faces in. They had never experienced anything like this before, to get kids out from a barricade and seat them off to the sides and give them water.'

You can see Lollapalooza's legacy in the way mosh pits have become an integral part of youth culture; beyond rock and metal, they're now firmly de rigueur in rap, too. But

Lollapalooza itself was losing its vigour. As early as 1995, Farrell admits: 'I just stopped caring. The worst thing that happened for me was that I lost the respect of the people who worked around me.'

Lollapalooza was revived as a single-site festival in 2005 and has taken over Grant Park in Chicago annually ever since. One recent year saw Lollapalooza host a T-Mobile stage, a Bud Light stage, a family-friendly zone called Kidzapalooza, and provide VIP and platinum ticketing options: platinum got you a concierge at the entrance and the chance to be driven in on a golf cart. There was no sign of any hemp or books on bomb-making.

From page 64, in order:
Trent Reznor performing with Nine Inch Nails, 1991
A crowd surfer silhouetted at sunset during a
    Lollapalooza tour stop, North Kingstown, 1993
Lollapalooza at Grant Park, Chicago, 2019

Electric Daisy Carnival

PLUR stands for peace, love, unity and respect. People show PLUR by exchanging bands of brightly coloured plastic beads known as Kandi. Despite looking like the kind of thing a six-year-old would nag a parent over, Kandi is the currency of PLUR, and both are the quirky, unique and intensely polarising byproducts of Electric Daisy Carnival – the EDM-championing US festival that changed the world in its wake.

EDC is not for everyone. It's not the kind of festival where you can rock up with a casual waterproof and amble around, catching a few bands, beer in hand. No, no, no. EDC is bright, brash, fast and hard. It's physically hard as well: its current location is Las Vegas Motor Speedway, so tarmac and concrete abound, though astroturf exists to cushion most flip-flopped footsteps. It's a voluminous festival, that scoops up young dance-music lovers from all over the country and gives them a place to run rampant and spread PLUR at the same time, soundtracked by the high priests of EDM: Tiësto, Steve Aoki, Calvin Harris, Diplo and Martin Garrix, to name a few.

When it began in 1999, EDC was a much more modest proposition and was totally shorn of its technicolor pomp. It was just 5,000 people in LA's Shrine Expo Hall, with a flyer that made it look like a psytrance event from the UK Home Counties. As EDC

About the festival

Location • Various locations wordwide (flagship is Las Vegas, Nevada, USA)

Started • 1991

Status • Still running

Notable headliners • Deadmau5, The Chainsmokers, David Guetta, Martin Garrix

Famous for • Remoulding raving for Middle America

Kindred spirits • Vh1 Supersonic, Ultra, Sonic Mania, Coachella

From left, in order:
A canopy of lights inside EDC, 2012
The stage at Tinker Field in Orlando, 2011
Day one of the festival in Orlando, 2017
Avicii fans in Las Vegas, 2011
The festival in full swing, 2017

'... it's grown into a haven of outlandish looks, furry boots, demented drug-related baby motifs and Kandi ...'

has grown into a haven of outlandish looks, demented drug-related baby motifs and Kandi, many European ravers have viewed all this juvenilia as hilariously old hat, given that they had already experienced a mainstream acid explosion years before. But in the mid-noughties, Americans were having their own second summer of love, fuelled by an upswing in drugs plus the active, pre-EDM blog house scene that saw dance music explode via the lawless, file-sharing development of the internet.

EDC founder Pasquale Rotella, described by *Billboard* as 'the Willy Wonka of EDM', said once that when someone disses PLUR in front of him, 'I just laugh and give those people a big hug, because they don't get it'. Yes, PLUR has a lot of amusing qualities – right down to the fact that one ONLY trades Kandi from the left arm, not the right. But EDM would be nothing without EDC, and the festival's growth to include sixteen countries, including England, Brazil, India and China, speaks volumes about how much of a success it has been.

KaZantip

Named after the beautifully circular Kazantyp cape in the north-eastern part of the Crimean peninsula, and lapped by the Sea of Azov, KaZantip was genuinely one of the most unusual festivals the world has ever seen.

The story begins in a derelict nuclear facility – the Crimean Atomic Energy Station – which was abandoned mid-construction following the Chernobyl disaster of 1986. An alternative energy source soon started flowing through the haunting and hulking concrete site, however. Between 1995 and 1999, the festival was more of an annual rave, with techno, trance and jungle pulsing through the solid walls and bare iron limbs of the deserted plant. Nearby beaches soothed comedowns for the young, hard-partying attendees.

Yet from the early 2000s, KaZantip adjusted into something even wilder and more decadent. Running over almost three weeks a year, the festival established itself in the beautiful village of Popovka and became both its own republic and a parody of the post-Soviet politics in the region. It had its own flag, for example, its own anthem (which was downloadable as a ringtone and for which you had to stand), and tickets were issued as visas. Some unruly attendees were even deported. It also had a semi-dictatorial leader as its head: President Nikita I, aka promoter Nikita Marshunok. But aside from the comedy value of declaring a stateless republic in a region that was itself part of a

About the festival

Location • Popovka, Crimea

Started • 1992

Status • Ended in 2014

Notable headliners • Carl Cox, Skrillex, Tiësto

Famous for • Becoming an actual state, not just a state of mind

Kindred spirits • Burning Man, Secret Garden Party, Lost & Found, Hideout

recently independent state, KaZantip really did have utopian hoop dreams. 'An attempt to create a new, improved society' no less, according to the glorious President Nikita. It may not have been a new Eden, but it was spiritually very close to America's Burning Man in its dedication to freedom, expression and artistic release.

On the flip side, a lot of people were unabashedly drawn to KaZantip by the fact that people mostly wore thongs and looked pretty hot 24/7. It wasn't as nakedly debauched as Burning Man, but for the region, it was positively scandalous. Another key difference to California's 'Burners' is that KaZantip boasted a far more egalitarian crowd. It may have counted billionaires among its loyal clientele, but the festival offered a chance for literally anybody to come for free. All they had to do was enter a contest to design a distinctive, fun, old-timey yellow suitcase and they were in, at the largesse of the dear leader.

Sadly, there's a bitter irony to the KaZantip story. What was styled as its own stateless and free domain fell victim to real world politics, as Russia's annexation of Crimea in 2014 forced the festival to seek alternative locations, and ultimately wind down and vanish.

'KaZantip was genuinely one of the most unusual festivals the world has ever seen.'

From page 72, in order:
On the beach, KaZantip, 2003
A couple smoking cigarettes, 2006
The nuclear power plant built in 1976 but never
    operated
Young lovers relax on the beach
A caravan turned drink shop
A view of the festival site next to the Black Sea

Big Day Out

The two men who started Australia's Big Day Out, Ken West and Vivian Lees, initially bonded while serving some low-level community service, after being arrested for putting up gig posters together. It's a cute origin story, and immediately hints at the slightly renegade past of the definitive coming-of-age festival experience of Australia's 90s and noughties youth.

'I hated that whole hippy bullshit concept,' Ken West once said. 'I wanted urban mayhem, I wanted controlled chaos, but I also wanted cold drinks, nice food, lots of choice, good drainage, lots of toilets and great production.'

Big Day Out started when the two promoters were putting on a tour of indie greats Violent Femmes in 1992. They'd taken a punt on an upcoming Seattle band, Nirvana, as support. In the intervening period, *Nevermind* exploded and the pair had a booking for the biggest band in the world in their back pocket. A one-day festival in Sydney was conceived, loads more bands were booked, and West ultimately changed the name from Kenfest to Big Day Out. Nirvana duly played and made about 10,000 kids pass out with excitement. A legend was born.

BDO quickly became a touring festival, tapping up Auckland, the Gold Coast, Sydney, Melbourne, Adelaide and Perth over two weeks, with the same bill of artists locked in for the journey. Some bands found this delightful. Others hated it. Some used it as a chance for romantic trysts with fellow touring acts (legal concerns prevent us

About the festival

Location • Multiple cities across Australia and New Zealand

Started • 1992

Status • Ended in 2014

Notable headliners • Nirvana, Iggy Pop, Tool, The Prodigy, The Killers

Famous for • Being ambitiously alternative

Kindred spirits • Reading Festival, T in the Park, Lovebox, Clockenflap

naming names, sorry dear reader), while others, such as Nick Cave in 1996, brought their current partners along. Of course, it helped that Nick's other half was Kylie Minogue, who would join him at each concert to duet their hit 'Where the Wild Roses Grow'.

Despite the terrible death of a concertgoer in 2001, Big Day Out continued to thrive throughout the noughties, bringing such huge names as The Killers, Pearl Jam, Muse, My Chemical Romance and Red Hot Chili Peppers to the tour. But as it grew into a behemoth, in 2011, original founder Lees bailed on the event. West partnered with the company behind that other great touring festival, Lollapalooza, which signalled a downturn in popularity among Australia's gig-goers. A creeping corporatisation, unhelpful staging and crowd control, and an unfriendly atmosphere (definitely not helped by the lack of any shade from the 40-degree heat at most sites) led to its demise, and Big Day Out was wrapped up in 2014. Today, in a bitter irony considering West's original views, it's staunchly hippie and smaller rural festivals known as bush doors that have the momentum again in Australia's festival scene. Be warned: never, ever dump on hippies.

'Nirvana duly played and made about 10,000 kids pass out with excitement. A legend was born.'

From page 76, in order:
Kurt Cobain of Nirvana plays the 1992 festival
Cooling down in Sydney, 2013
Ticket from 2008; poster from 1992
Crowd surfing, 1995
Iggy Pop onstage in 1993

Sziget

This festival's origins are rooted in the fall of the Soviet Union at the tail end of the 1980s. Hungary's Communist state had previously provided both arts and cultural funding, as well as activities such as summer youth camps. The student organisers who began the festival in 1993 wanted to bridge that gap, and, rather perfectly, they ended up doing it on a site that literally requires a bridge to access it.

In northern Budapest sits Óbudai-sziget, the largest Danubian island in the Hungarian capital. What formed as an accumulation of debris from the fast-flowing Danube would become home to a Roman legion circa 89 CE, was used as a carrot farm as late as 1960, and today hosts possibly one of the most lavish and varied festivals in the world.

Sziget is huge. It lasts for seven days and during its epic annual August stint, around 400,000 'sziticens' walk over the bridge onto the island to enjoy a truly starry cast of headliners (Kendrick Lamar, Prince, Foo Fighters and Florence and the Machine are just some celebrated bill-toppers). Such is its status as a destination festival that organisers claim it packs in over 100 nationalities of visitor a year. Like Glastonbury, it promotes entertainment of the most imaginative, only-at-a-festival kind: there's an annual procession of cardboard art, a whole on-site village dedicated to Hungarian culture (with loads of dancing), and bookings that include anything from primate expert Jane Goodall to a company of male dancers who perform in the nude.

About the festival

Location • Óbudai-sziget, northern Budapest, Hungary

Started • 1992

Status • Still running

Notable headliners • R.E.M. Prince, Blur, Dua Lipa

Famous for • Its iconic island setting and the fact it goes on for seven whole days!

Kindred spirits • Bestival, Benicàssim, Bonnaroo, Open'er, Melt

And for anyone who gets too steamy, or indeed covered in dust from the occasional-but-notable dust storms, there's also a beach on the island – of course.

Older readers may well remember it being called Pepsi Sziget. This was simply because one of the first incarnations – Diáksziget (Student's Island) – went so spectacularly over budget that organisers had to sell naming rights to the festival until 2002 to pay off those initial debts. Since then, it's been a stable ship, and almost a novelty in festival land for never having to change location. Sziget's subtitle is 'Island of Freedom', but between ten stages of acts, a majorly friendly and positive crowd, PLUS the occasional boat party, most sane people would choose the island over freedom any day.

'... most sane people would choose the island over freedom any day.'

From page 80, in order:
Feeling the love, 2018
Sziget ticket from 2006
Chilling out
The crowd soaking up the atmosphere in 2018
Throwing beach balls at the 2017 festival
Audience interaction in 2017

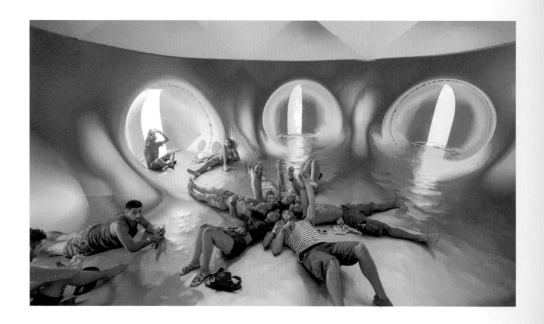

Sónar

Festivals are magical little snowflake-shaped entities because, unlike, say, a Diet Coke, you cannot enjoy the exact same festival in different parts of the world. They're rooted in a place. There's one glaring exception to this rule, however: Sónar, the Barcelona-born bae of the electronic dance scene, which has proved the most exportable festival in the world.

It began back in 1994, when a trio of enthusiasts including a music journalist (see, we're not a completely useless bunch) assembled a mixed platter of contemporary underground dance musicians for a three-day festival. Even in 1994, Sónar had its most distinctive feature locked in: a split between day and night, across two completely different sites. Sónar by Day was for years held amidst gleaming cultural centres CCCB and MACBA, but has since relocated to the huge exhibition spaces of Fira de Barcelona. As a variety of outdoor stages play magnificent dance music, Europe's most discerning aficionados of all things hntz-hntz gather on artificial grass in the blazing sun, drink booze steadily all day and still retain a respectable air of cultured hipsterdom.

After sundown, and maybe a disco siesta, comes Sónar by Night. A whole different festival site beckons, the jumbo Fira Gran Via L'Hospitalet. Where daytime was in the city centre, nighttime is in the outskirts – for very good reason. Some of the loudest sonic visionaries have preached their glitchy gospel at Sónar by Night, including Boys Noize, Daft Punk, Aphex Twin, SOPHIE, and more. The

vast rooms hum and throb until 7am, when the music winds down and ravers respectfully integrate into the city's metro system.

London was the first city outside of Spain to be blessed with Sónar's expert curation. Since 2002, Sónar has held events in a staggering sixty-five cities across four different continents. Truly the Diet Coke of festivals.

About the festival

Location • Barcelona, Spain

Started • 1994

Status • Still running

Notable headliners • Kraftwerk, Laurent Garnier, Nicolas Jaar, Skrillex, The Chemical Brothers

Famous for • Fostering the most civilised dance music fans in the world

Kindred spirits • Dekmantel, MUTEK, AVA Festival, Amsterdam Dance Event, Time Warp, Labyrinth Festival

Left:
Chemical Brothers onstage, 2015

Fuji Rock

Let's get the obvious thing out of the way first: no, Fuji Rock does not take place in Fuji. It did once, in its inaugural outing in 1997, at the foot of the great mountain. But it was a bit of a disaster. A typhoon terrorised an unprepared crowd. Many developed hypothermia and the second day was scrapped. Two years later, though, it found its home: 150 miles away, at the Naeba ski resort, which isn't exactly known for its easygoing weather either.

Fuji Rock is synonymous with ponchos, such is the festival's insane proclivity for rain. Located a forty-minute train ride from Tokyo, the mountains of Niigata become the annual soggy playground for multiple generations of Japanese music fans. Like Glastonbury, Fuji scoops up loyal, repeat visitors who attend habitually, even when they've settled into parenthood. Fear not, though, as the festival has come to accommodate kids handsomely over the years. 'One of my dreams,' stated festival runner Masahiro Hidaka, 'is to have three generations of family coming to the festival, and enjoying – or criticising – the music they like with each other.'

The fact that Fuji Rock draws comparisons to Glastonbury is perhaps no surprise. Hidaka, who himself grew up in mountains, began on the path to Fuji Rock with an anti-nuclear event called Atomic Cafe, meeting Glastonbury's Michael Eavis along the way. A deeply rebellious soul, Hidaka fought to establish the festival in a society that was still highly conservative

About the festival

Location • Niigata Prefecture, Japan

Started • 1997

Status • Still running

Notable headliners • Gorillaz, Oasis, Run-DMC

Famous for • Rain, rain and more rain!

Kindred spirits • Glastonbury, WOMAD, Pukkelpop, Øya Festival, Meadows in the Mountains

From left, in order:
Tents on site for Fuji Rock, 2014
Posters from 2019 and 2017
Pure nature at Naeba ski resort, 2008
Beneath the mountains, crowds move from stage to stage between acts, 2008
In the rain, 2008

and restrictive to alternative culture. Yet ironically, perhaps, Fuji Rock's most distinctive feature is itself deeply emblematic of the best aspect of Japanese culture: its intense cleanliness.

Fuji Rock is famous for its lack of rubbish. Where just about any other festival ground in the world would be a sea of cups, cans and fags once the music had finished, Fuji Rock maintains its lush, verdant grass floor all weekend long. Organisers are so committed to there being no waste that kind human guides exist on site to show punters which of the myriad recycling bins to use. This ethos makes sense on a site like Naeba, a total monster of a setting, which runs to four kilometres of pure nature. Walking between stages involves some very beautiful trails, but their hilliness is not for the faint-hearted. Fortunately, visitors can take stock of it all by riding the Dragondola – Japan's longest cable car – which offers incredible views from its destination at the top of the mountain over the whole festival site. And while a great many of the ski hotels nearby accommodate the bulk of festival-goers, more die-hard ravers can set up camp at an on-site campsite. Just make sure your tent is pegged down lest another typhoon hits.

Lilith Fair

In Jewish mythology, before Adam and Eve, there was Adam and Lilith. Lilith was the first wife of Adam, who refused to be dominated by him and fled the Garden of Eden. Lilith Fair, a pioneering American festival that ran between 1997 and 1999, was an attempt to flee the male orthodoxies of the music industry, which at the time were bone-headed to say the least.

The main spur for a festival of female solo artists and female-led bands was simple: women in music were still treated as novelties, curiosities and funny little counterpoints to the big boys of the industry. As a maddening result, promoters never put more than one woman on a concert bill. Similarly, radio stations would rarely playlist more than one woman at a time. In the words of singer-songwriter and festival co-founder Sarah McLachlan: 'They'd say, "We added Tori Amos this week, so we can't add you." Or: "We added Tracy Chapman this week, so we can't add you." And I'm like, "We're doing completely different [things]!"'

Factor in what critic Chris Molanphy called 'bro-fication of alternative rock' at the time, and it was clear to many that a change was required. Lilith Fair did something different. It was a festival by women, for women. Men could respectfully attend, of course – or guest, as a guitar-toting Prince did during a Sheryl Crow set in 1999 – but it was meant as as a female-focused event at its core. It was a way of proving that a brace of acts – Indigo Girls, Jewel, Emmylou Harris, Natalie Merchant,

About the festival

Location • Various cities across the USA and Canada

Started • 1997

Status • Ended in 2010

Notable headliners • Sarah McLachlan, Suzanne Vega, Tracy Chapman, Sheryl Crow

Famous for • Finally putting women first

Kindred spirits • Girls Just Wanna Weekend, LOUD WOMEN Fest, California Women's Music

India Arie, Fiona Apple and more – had market appeal. And lo, the first Lilith Fair grossed $16 million.

To the distraction of the organisers, the festival revealed a textbook set of double standards, held up to women but never to their male equivalents. People taking a shot at Lilith Fair pointed, for example, to a lack of diversity on the bill. As McLachlan reflected years later: 'We got a lot of flak for being a white-chick folk fest.' But, she added, 'I don't think Perry Farrell was taken to task for those things' when he was assembling Lollapalooza. In fact, in the two years after its debut, Lilith Fair managed to feature Missy Elliott, Queen Latifah, Lauryn Hill and Neneh Cherry. It was revived in 2010, with Janelle Monáe joining the fair among others, but for a host of reasons it didn't smash the box office as it once had and McLachlan wrapped up the festival that year for good. 'White-chick folk' didn't age all that well, and by the start of the 2000s, pop and R&B had come to hijack the narrative. But in terms of giving the male-run music industry a bracing kick up the backside, Lilith Fair will always be a shining light.

From page 90, in order:
Sarah McLachlan onstage, 1998
Poster from the first Lilith Fair
Sinead O'Connor performing, 1997
Jewel takes the stage in 1997
The audience at Canterbury Park in Shakopee, 1998

'Lilith Fair did something different. It was a festival by women, for women.'

Melt

If you had access to something known as 'the city of iron' – aka an entire peninsula that acted solely as a museum of gigantic metal machinery – you'd host a massive festival there too. Right?

And lo it came to be that the awesomely named Ferropolis – a vast open-air heritage space in the German town of Gräfenhainichen – plays host to one of the most kick-ass festivals in Europe. Just don't ask for anything as trite as heavy metal: Melt is an encapsulation of the finest and most on-point bands and DJs, set in a dystopic, rusty and dusty adult playground.

Among the giant, looming, over-arching mining machinery on the horizon, Melt offers huge names, twenty-four-hour programming, and a spirited and communal vibe among its roughly 20,000 visitors every year. The many highlights of the site include the Big Wheel stage, which integrates nicely with the hulking machines, as it harbours a giant rave-up next to them and acts as the most robust speaker stand the world has ever seen. Then there's the legendary Sleepless Floor stage, which somehow never stops for the entire duration (that's a full ninety-odd hours). German techno hero Ellen Allien has become a de facto resident and icon of the stage, her sets often charged with drawing the marathon techno feat to a close. Melt also boasts a late-night forest, which houses a lake-straddling stage offering beautiful views of the surrounding Lake Gremmin, and the Secret Garden of Porn – a queer performance space with an

About the festival

Location • Gräfenhainichen, Germany

Started • 1997

Status • Still running

Notable headliners • Oasis, Portishead, Björk

Famous for • The audacious industrial machines that define the Melt experience

Kindred spirits • Burning Man, Arcadia, Flow Festival

From left, in order:
Couple skipping through the festival
A floating panda joins in with the festivities
People gather to watch a band in the evening
The crowd enjoy the evening action
'The city of iron' plays host to the festival each year

obviously salacious name but the clout of Berlin performance crew Pornceptual to back it up.

As if to reinforce an allegiance to the most emblematic form of techno travel, there's also a dedicated train service running to Melt. This is an overnight fandango, which sets off from Cologne and of course features DJs, a club carriage and 600 pumped-up people on their festival pre-game. It joins other dedicated festival trains past and present, such as the RockNess Express, as being the most raucous train journey since locomotion began and generally elevates Melt to the pantheon of festivals.

'Melt is an encapsulation of the finest and most on-point bands and DJs, set in a dystopic, rusty and dusty adult playground.'

Tuska

Are you a fan of mosh circles that are hairy in both senses of the word? Well, Finnish metal festival Tuska should be right up your street. When it comes to having something for every metaller, Tuska is the definitive rock banger by the Baltic Sea.

Tuska began in 1998, after metal magazine *Suomi Finland Perkele* pitched the idea of a festival dedicated to the dark arts of Finnish music impresario Juhani Merimaa. By year three it had become an event catering for 5,000 Finns at a time. By year four, that figure had grown to 10,000. Having burned through a few different sites in its infancy, Tuska Open Air Metal Festival (to give it its full title) settled on its long-term home in 2011, having reached the heady heights of drawing in 28,000 fans a year. This was Suvilahti: a former power plant in Helsinki, which now also plays host to Flow Festival. Three stages of well-curated metal and rock are Tuska's core draw, and though they've been blessed with such huge names as Alice Cooper, Slayer, Megadeth and Napalm Death as headliners in the past, as with many northern European festivals, the experience is often more about discovery than anything else. Look beyond the main stage and Tuska bleeds a sense of fun, too. Yes, demonic face make-up, flame-belching pyrotechnics and some truly scary fonts might be part of the schtick, but on the flip side there's an on-site sauna, you can drink out of medieval horns, and you can even get your clothes cleaned and laundered. Rock. And. Roll.

About the festival

Location • Helsinki, Finland

Started • 1998

Status • Still running

Notable headliners • Korn, Slayer, Deftones, Anthrax

Famous for • Dark rock played under blue skies

Kindred spirits • Download, Rock am Ring, Hellfest, Rock Werchter

From left, in order:
Metal fans at Tuska, 2019
A former power plant forms the backdrop for the festival
Trivium onstage in 2012
The crowd enjoy deathcore band Suicide Silence, 2012
Polish death metal band Behemoth onstage, 2012

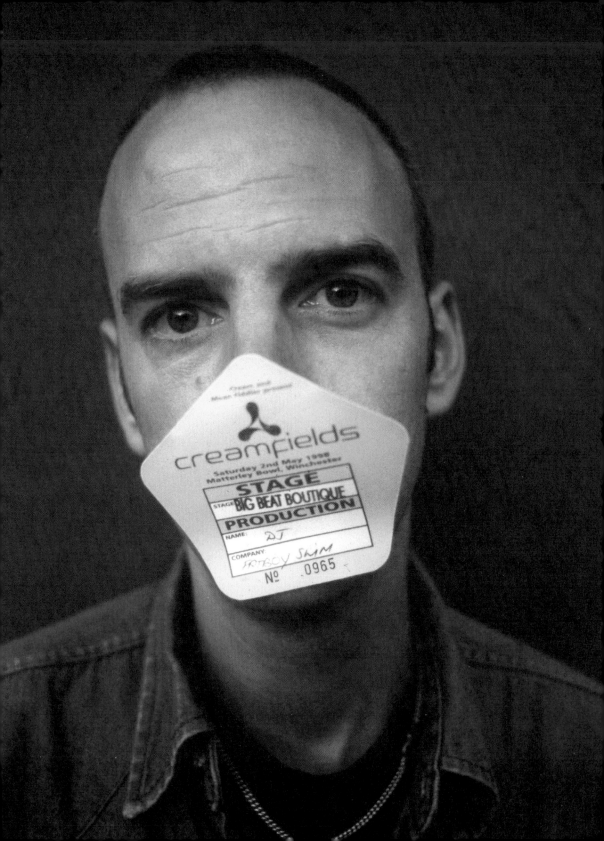

Creamfields

A nightclub running a festival? Sounds normal and run-of-the-mill today, but back in the 90s, the link between clubland and festival-land was far, far wider.

While live-ish dance music makers like The Orb, Orbital and The Chemical Brothers were starting to place high on the bills of conventional music fests by the mid-90s, there wasn't a similar place for club-rocking DJs at the time, despite their ability to bring in punters to some of the biggest clubs in the UK, week-on-week.

Most nascent dance festivals at the time, such as Tribal Gathering, had come out of the free party scene. But in contrast to the hard-edged and uncompromising vibes of the early acid house days of outdoor raving, Creamfields' first outing, in Winchester in 1998, signified a shift into a different dimension. As an extension of the Liverpool club, festival-goers would express themselves by being glam, glitzy and, literally, fluffy (boas and fluffy bras were de rigueur back then). It also represented a move from clubs being rooted in bricks-and-mortar venues to being seen as 'brands'.

That first ever Creamfields changed the scene in a big way. The line-up packed some heavy-hitting live acts, such as Run-DMC, Primal Scream, and a young and then hair-raisingly techno Daft Punk. But despite being held in Winchester – hundreds of miles from the club's hometown – the bulk of the bill consisted of DJs allied to the house aesthetic of the Cream sound. Sasha, Paul van Dyk, Pete Tong, Carl Cox, Cajmere,

About the festival

Location • Winchester/Cheshire, UK

Started • 1998

Status • Still running

Notable headliners • Daft Punk, The Chemical Brothers, Avicii, The Prodigy

Famous for • Being the first club brand to set themselves up as a festival

Kindred spirits • Defected Festival, Tribal Gathering, KISSTORY, Global Gathering

Paul Oakenfold and Fatboy Slim were just some of the names playing until 6am – and all remained festival headliners for two decades after this first field-based foray.

Creamfields was embryonic in creating the notion of the dance music festival. Everything from Tomorrowland to Coachella to Electric Daisy Carnival owes a debt to Creamfields, which still carries on today – albeit with fewer fluffy bras.

Left:
Fatboy Slim aka Norman Cook backstage, 1998

Iceland Airwaves

Let's consider the many ways in which Reykjavik's Iceland Airwaves, a twenty-plus-year veteran of the Euro fest scene, is pretty damn different from the rest.

Well, for starters, it's the world's most northerly festival, and is thus mercilessly freezing given that (another big difference incoming) it's held annually in November. That's around the period when the youthful population of Reykjavik is exposed to just a few hours of sunlight every day. There's hardly a flip-flop in sight, basically.

Another key difference: it's all indoors. Which is lucky, as it frequently buckets down. But don't let any of this faze you – these factors actually work in favour of a festival built on discovery, variety and a whole lot of roaming. All backdropped by the genuinely epic peninsulas, coves and islands that surround this breathtaking city.

The first incarnation of the festival, back in 1999, was held in a giant airplane hangar at Reykjavik Airport. While the festival's sponsor, Icelandair, has remained, the format of the festival has shifted drastically. Iceland Airwaves is known and loved as a serving platter of music spread over a host of different venues – be they large concert halls, clubs, museums, bars, and even the odd ornate church or two. One wristband gives punters access to every venue, all located within walking distance of each other.

About the festival

Location • Reykjavik, Iceland

Started • 1999

Status • Still running

Notable headliners • Mac DeMarco, Fleet Foxes, Biffy Clyro, Metronomy

Famous for • Being a multi-venue haven for alternative music

Kindred spirits • Land of Kings, Camden Crawl, South by Southwest, Nuits Sonores, Field Day, All Points East

From left, in order:
Enjoying a drink in the Blue Lagoon
Frikirkjan Church becomes a concert venue as part of the festival, 2017
Ólafur Arnalds performing in the National Theatre, 2018
The crowd take in the atmosphere whilst Of Monsters and Men perform, 2019
Kiasmos performing in 2017

It's very much intended as a showcase of both big established names, such as Yoko Ono, Florence and the Machine, Beach House, Robyn and Björk, and a litany of up-coming, gleefully alternative Scandinavian talent, too. Over the years this has ranged from the chillwave balladry of Norwegian singer Sigrid to bombastic folk-rock from Of Monsters and Men and even a full-on rave assault by Sweden's Slagsmålsklubben, whose name translates as 'fight club'. Rest assured though, Reykjavik's music-loving, hip-as-hell hosts never let Iceland Airwaves descend into anything other than a total love-in of alternative music.

'Iceland Airwaves is known and loved as a serving platter of music spread over a host of different venues — be they large concert halls, clubs, museums, bars, and even the odd ornate church or two.'

Coachella

Most people hated the name 'Coachella' when Paul Tollett first floated the idea of holding a music festival in the Californian desert, in the city of Indio. That wasn't even the full name. The concert promoter in fact wished to call it the 'Coachella Valley Music and Arts Festival'.

Tollett and his coterie from Goldenvoice Productions were bursting with enthusiasm to make something happen, having run shows on the 90s punk and grunge scene, and then seen the rise of outdoor raves and British-influenced electronica later the same decade. Friends and colleagues had also travelled across Europe's festival scene and were imagining the buzz, fervour and spirit of an event like Glastonbury but with actual Californian sun.

On a site-for-site comparison, Glastonbury's Pilton Farm could not be more different to the Empire Polo Club in Indio, California. There's no mud, and certainly no bovine waste to speak of in the desert. By contrast, attendees to the first ever Coachella in 1999 were shocked to feel fresh, manicured grass underfoot for the whole day. They were also blasted by 100°F heat, which made the festival switch in subsequent years from October to the cooler month of April – a switch that would pay off for myriad reasons later on.

From the earliest years, Coachella became synonymous with reunions. In its make or break second year, with a crowd-pulling headliner nowhere to be found, the organisers reached out to Jane's Addiction

About the festival

Location • California, USA

Started • 1999

Status • Still running

Notable headliners • OutKast, Pixies, Beyoncé, Childish Gambino, Prince, Ariana Grande, Lady Gaga, Daft Punk

Famous for • Coaxing the retired and reluctant back onstage, year after year

Kindred spirits • Glastonbury, Lollapalooza, Wireless, Benicàssim

to reunite. The pivotal moment, though, was the Pixies reunion in 2004. Here was a band whose singer, Black Francis, quit by fax in 1993 (yes, that dates it nicely, doesn't it). It was such a unique thing to offer festival crowds that it started the association of the desert fest as a place for genuine, one-off marvels.

And the moments just kept happening … Amidst a revival of post-punk, Brit-goths Bauhaus were persuaded to reform in 2005 with singer Peter Murphy entering the stage dangled upside down from a hoist to sing 'Bela Lugosi's Dead'. Rage Against The Machine reformed to tear up the main stage in 2007, while in later years OutKast teamed up for the event in 2014, as did Guns N' Roses and LCD Soundsystem in 2016. The only elusive band for Tollett and his team seemed to be The Smiths, with two reported overtures (and big money amounts) made to Morrissey and Marr to no avail.

But reunions are far from the only story. Coachella has been able to coax out some of the most mind-blowing performances from the last twenty years, making April a fixture in the calendar akin to the State of the Union address. Daft Punk's 2006 performance changed America. Period. The French duo not only reignited their own career with a stage show that encapsulated their previously eccentric desire to be robots, but it also led to the explosion of EDM and other forms of dance music in America; a testament to the fact that spectacle could carry a DJ to the upper echelons of a line-up. Less remembered but just as epochal: Madonna played the Sahara Tent (aka the dancey one) that same year, armed with recent LP *Confessions on a Dance Floor*, and became the first genuine megastar to play the festival, coolly doing it in a hothouse tent.

Other big moments include MIA taking America hostage with an amazing set at what was her first-ever festival in 2005, or Jay-Z opening his hastily arranged replacement set for the Beastie Boys with a note-perfect 'No Sleep Till Brooklyn'. Another hip hop legend who couldn't make Coachella was Tupac, due to his having died in 1996. Regardless, he appeared during Snoop and Dr Dre's headline set in hologram form (actually a process known as Pepper's Ghost), breaking the internet in the process. And then there was Beychella – Beyoncé's triumphant 2018 headline set – which served as much as historical insight (into the place of Black American college culture) as headliner entertainment, putting her into the auteur category of performer, in the mould of Kate Bush and David Byrne.

Coachella is that rarest of things: a huge, money-rich commercial enterprise that somehow still manages to represent the peak of artistic expression year-after-year – despite the terrible name.

From page 108, in order:
2019 Coachella festival style
California sunset, 2014
Flower power in 2019
Beyoncé headlines in 2018
Poolside fashion launch as part of the festival, 2018
Sculptures and sun in 2017
Coachella festival grounds, 2019

Splendour in the Grass

Surely anyone who has done a festival to the absolute max will agree that sometimes only classical poetry can really do it justice? Consider Wordsworth's 'Intimations of Immortality': 'Though nothing can bring back the hour/Of splendour in the grass, glory in the flower/We will grieve not; rather find/Strength in what remains behind.'

Making incredible memories while we're young is what festivals are all about. And it's fitting that Wordsworth should inspire the name of a festival that has slowly conquered the Australian scene since its inception in 2001.

Occupying the space that Big Day Out once did for a younger generation, with similarly wide-eyed musical tastes and thirsts for adventure, Splendour has bounced around different locations such as Byron Bay, New South Wales and Woodford in Queensland. It has since settled at North Byron Parklands in Yelgun, New South Wales. Lush is a generally overused word, but Parklands is a genuinely verdant space: 660 acres located close to the coast and blessed with its own centrepiece amphitheatre. This natural bowl shape in the landscape is the obvious locale for the main stage, which in turn is blessed with the absolute pick of the global A-list every year. Those who have previously been splendid at Splendour include Kendrick Lamar, Lorde, Kanye West, Arctic Monkeys and Tame Impala.

About the festival

Location • Byron Shire and Woodford, Australia

Started • 2001

Status • Still running

Notable headliners • Coldplay, Kendrick Lamar, Gorillaz, Tame Impala, Lorde

Famous for • Line-ups in a perfect space

Kindred spirits • Big Day Out, Wilderness, Latitude, Blissfields

From left, in order:
Crowds descend on Byron Bay for Splendour in the Grass, 2018
Festival-goers relax at the Amphitheatre stage as the sun sets, 2019
Watching Wolfmother perform in 2019
Childish Gambino onstage, 2019
Making their way to the music

The GW McLennan tent (named after the sadly deceased co-founder of The Go-Betweens) tends to play host to massive homegrown talent, who often out-sparkle the big-name imports, while elsewhere on site you can run the gamut from a buskers stage to a champagne bar. Not that Splendour is a haven of inequality. It was in fact one of the first festivals to act when ticket touts began buying up big chunks of allocations and selling them on for vastly inflated prices. In 2006, a year ahead of Glastonbury, the festival took the then-novel step of registering purchasers, so that their names appeared on the tickets. Both now suffer from such rabid popularity that anyone not primed and ready to spend at 9am will not get a ticket. But for the kind of proper splendour that may make memories, it's a pain worth putting up with.

'Making incredible memories while we're young is what festivals are all about.'

Primavera Sound

Few festivals provoke such intense feelings of raw, angst-inducing desire as Barcelona's Primavera Sound. Each year's line-up announcement is like a beautifully orchestrated campaign to get every cool, music-loving European to sigh deeply in awe. It really is just that good. What began as a small, 7,000-capacity festival in 2001 has blossomed into an agenda-setting, zeitgeist-defining love letter to alternative music.

Let's burst some bubbles right away. Primavera isn't *completely* perfect. There's one aspect above all that rankles, and it's to do with ankles. Specifically the pounding they take on the almost exclusively concrete setting of Parc del Fòrum, the country's largest urban park and home to the waterside festival since 2005. Naturally, no tent pegs are going in without a pneumatic drill, so all the accommodation is off site. But with the knowledge that a proper bed is only a cab ride away for most punters, Primavera goes later than many 'proper camping' fests. It's known for putting on the finest dance music across all genres until around 6am. And while it gets a decent number of fair-weather fans and party-chasers, Primavera really does engender the same form of intense muso love that compels people to get a Sonic Youth tattoo on their boob.

About the festival

Location • Barcelona, Spain

Started • 2001

Status • Still running

Notable headliners • Neil Young, Arcade Fire, My Bloody Valentine, Patti Smith, Brian Wilson

Famous for • Line-ups that make other festivals jealous

Kindred spirits • Sónar, Meltdown, Field Day

Listing the music that has been performed at Primavera represents the majority of the alternative canon of Western music. Patti Smith's 'Horses'? Performed in full. Neil Young, Van Morrison? Check, check. Ditto Lou Reed, Brian Wilson and Iggy Pop. Radiohead? Of course. The Fall, Pixies, My Bloody Valentine, Aphex Twin? All smashed it (and eardrums, too). And with a 2019 commitment to booking a 50–50 male–female split already behind them, many more women will hopefully join this list very soon. Long may the online FOMO continue.

'It's known for putting on the finest dance music across all genres until around 6am.'

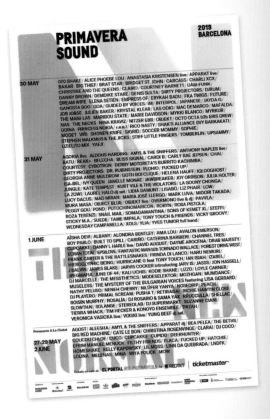

From page 118, in order:
FKA Twigs performs in 2019
Radiohead onstage, 2016
The line-up for 2019
Festival-goers enjoy a Barcelona sunset
The audience at Parc del Fòrum, 2012
The crowd gathers in 2013

AfrikaBurn

In terms of sheer ease, South Africa's AfrikaBurn must surely rank as one of the most inconvenient gatherings imaginable. It's a survivalist's paradise and a glamper's worst nightmare. Most festivals, say, don't insist punters bring spare tyres for the treacherous journey to the site. Access is mostly via an airstrip which WILL turn away any planes wanting to land past 5pm. Dry and extremely hot during the day, yet bitterly cold at night, at AfrikaBurn water is unobtainable, yet perversely the only thing for sale is ice …

To add more nuance, AB rejects the label of being a straight music festival, and views its content more as a coming together of individual sound systems run by attendees, a bit like the pervading 'amateur' spirit of the modern Olympics. This is not a classic headliner festival by any means. Yet without the anxiety of having to race around trying to catch bands playing all weekend, the pace of AfrikaBurn allows events like the incredible sunrises in the middle of the Karoo to occupy the headliner slot. Art, sculpture and all manner of creative endeavours are huge, again expressed through the decentralised structure of the festival – which dictates that everyone has to get involved in some way, shape or form – and the latent flamboyance of attendees. Pistonheads convert cars into giant snails and pirate ships. By contrast, an incredible 100-foot structure named Subterrafuge protested fracking in 2014 – one of many works to have a more obviously political genesis.

About the festival

Location • Northern Cape, South Africa

Started • 2001

Status • Still running

Notable headliners • The art is always the headliner, darling…

Famous for • Being the African iteration of Burning Man

Kindred spirits • Burning Man

From left, in order:
Effigy in the desert, AfrikaBurn 2019
Structures spring up in the Karoo, 2016
Sculptural platform, 2018
Enormous creations destined to be set alight
Burning man, 2018

AfrikaBurn is the largest of Burning Man's 130 regionally affiliated events, though at 5,000 attendees it is still only a tenth of the Nevada mothership's size and capacity. Yet many look to AfrikaBurn as the beating spirit of BM, before the American iteration became tainted by mainstream popularity and Silicon Valley yuppies. What makes AfrikaBurn so uniquely unique, despite the almost insane trek to get there, are the star-speckled skies above the Karoo desert and the intense swirls of pink and purple hues that frame the decadent partying below.

'Many look to AfrikaBurn as the beating spirit of BM, before the American iteration became tainted by mainstream popularity ...'

Lovebox

If Lovebox proves anything, it's that all festivals should be born from a party.

Rarely for a festival, this long-running one-day London institution was also birthed by musicians: UK dance duo Groove Armada, whose signature numbers include 'At the River', 'I See You Baby' and the reggaefied house classic 'Superstylin''.

The two men behind Groove Armada, Tom Findlay and Andy Cato, conceived of the festival as a celebration of their east-London-centered club night, Lovebox. A park on the other side of town, the genteel Clapham Common, was picked as the location for its inaugural outing. Having actual dance musicians at the helm meant that it had a DJ slant. In fact, Lovebox earned a great reputation by making dance music a daytime delight again, rather than something that belonged in the dark of night. Among the great DJ auteurs to have played are Frankie Knuckles, DJ Harvey, Gilles Peterson and Norman Jay MBE.

Lovebox really came into its own after moving to the Hackney-straddling Victoria Park in 2005. At the time, east London neighbourhoods like Hackney, Shoreditch and Hoxton were going through an explosion of creativity and easy-to-mock hipster cool. Yet while Lovebox was able to tap into that energy (some of the defining names from the noughties passed through the Tower Hamlets site, such as The Flaming Lips, Goldfrapp, Friendly Fires and N*E*R*D), it was the talent on its own doorstep that really gave it character.

About the festival

Location • London, UK

Started • 2002

Status • Still running

Notable headliners • Grace Jones, MIA, Chase & Status, LCD Soundsystem, Solange

Famous for • Bringing London's queer scene into the festival spotlight

Kindred spirits • British Summer Time, Parklife, Mighty Hoopla, Wireless, Field Day

From left, in order:
Dancing in the tent, 2015
Lovebox line-up, 2018
Onstage at the Lost Vagueness Arena, 2005
Grace Jones performs, 2010
Fans soak up the atmosphere as Groove Armada perform, 2008

London's East End drag scene was in the midst of a renaissance, a total wig-wearing, lipstick-smudging, bar-straddling moment. So from 2010, Lovebox Sunday became a home for homos, a camp festival without any camping. Sunday became 'gay day'. In 2010, Grace Jones, Peaches, Hercules and Love Affair all played. Glastonbury's queer palace, NYC Downlow – now regarded as 'the greatest club in the world' – was also set up at Lovebox that year, resplendent in its derelict brilliance, with glamourpusses deftly teasing potential punters. London icon Jonny Woo assembled the talent and bled stages with a marauding group of performers, all taking the straight edges off a traditional festival experience. What accounted for the raw appeal of his trannie coterie? As he told *Time Out* in 2012, 'We're better dressed, we've got more staying power and we're always up for a shag at the end of it. Even if you haven't washed.'

In later years, Lovebox would move to west London's Gunnersbury Park and embrace a much younger demographic of hip hop, grime and experimental R&B fans. Gay day ebbed away, but its role in queering the UK festival scene proudly remains.

'... Lovebox earned a great reputation by making dance music a daytime delight again ...'

Nuits Sonores

The marriage of dance music and post-industrial space is a happy, timeless union that never gets dull or goes out of fashion. It's a formula that has been working beautifully since the 80s, since the acid house explosion, since Frankie Knuckles forged house music at Chicago's Warehouse. And at French festival Nuits Sonores, that special bond continues to thrive.

Lyon is a famously beautiful city, yet there's another side to the UNESCO World Heritage site that is exploited cannily by this dance-focused fest. Similar to Barcelona's Sónar, Nuits Sonores splits itself over day and night sessions. Former sugar storage facility La Sucrière, located on the banks of the Saône, is where the daytime action takes place. These are mostly events curated by single artists, such as Bonobo, Peggy Gou and Jeff Mills, who then play a headline set at the end of it all. Night action then moves to the old Fagor-Brandt factories, where a warren of warehouses plays host to everyone from Bicep and Maceo Plex to French party king Laurent Garnier. What really sets this festival apart, though, is the sheer chutzpah of the length of it all. Some years it's lasted eight or nine days in total, a Herculean effort for any festival, yet luckily, year after year, the crowds seem as solid as the great hulking structures that define Nuits Sonores.

About the festival

Location • Lyon, France

Started • 2003

Status • Still running

Notable headliners • James Blake, DJ Harvey, Nina Kraviz

Famous for • Being one of the few festivals that works indoors

Kindred spirits • Sónar, Iceland Airwaves, Dekmantel

Left:
Lost in music, 2009

Bang Face Weekender

What started in 2003 as a one-off party has become a nurturing community of like-minded idiot rave geniuses who will gently donk any form of seriousness on the head with a giant inflatable banana to the sound of a 200bpm face-melting techno screech. Welcome to Bang Face ...

Bang Face Weekender, which evolved from a long-running London club night, is delicately hard to describe. It's silly, it's voluminous, it's a sea of inflatables, dayglo and people dressed as kids' TV characters of old (did an eight-person Thomas The Tank Engine costume just walk past?). It's an affectionate and very over the top pastiche of early rave culture. Most crucially, it's a place to go completely and utterly nuts and have the most fun imaginable.

Some of the music you might hear – genres like gabber, happy hardcore, breakcore – may sound inherently jokey to many, yet there are loyal devotees of the extreme sounds of rave, and Bang Face is there for them. Yes, a lot of the bill is closer to surrealist comedy than the conventional DJ (take DJ Scotch Egg, who plays using a Game Boy or two), but there is also a deep love of wild, innovative and cleverly punishing music, and such godlike people as Aphex Twin and Jeff Mills have passed through the stages too, as well as

About the festival

Location • Southport, UK

Started • 2003

Status • Still running

Notable headliners • Aphex Twin, Venetian Snares, Altern-8, Jeff Mills, The Orb, Vengaboys

Famous for • Finding the sweet spot between being witty and silly

Kindred spirits • All Tomorrow's Parties, Bloc Weekend

'Humour shoots through everything to do with Bang Face.'

the kings and queens of acid, jungle and old-school rave.

Bang Face really is one of the most passionate, audience-driven events around. The community is there every step of the way. The fans, known as Hard Crew, get the vibe and join in. It all looks very, very wrong from the outside, and maybe it is, but it's also a massive laugh at the same time.

It first mutated from a club to a festival in 2008 and now runs annually in spring at a traditional British holiday camp built for traditional family holidays in Southport, Merseyside. It's a heaven-made match of weird people in a weird setting, with the kidult mentality making good use of the camp's swimming pool, go-karting circuit and army of arcade games (which, all clustered together and chirping, sound uncannily like the mashed-up techno equals inside the arenas).

Humour shoots through everything to do with Bang Face. It makes brilliant use of abstract statements and lol slogans, printed onto banners and left for the crowd to hold and wave. 'You can't really communicate in a rave,' said Bang Face founder St Acid in 2019. 'It's so loud, so you find a banner that represents your mood. That became more and more abstract, and sillier, so now people are just holding up total nonsense. But it means everything to them.'

Each chalet within Pontins has its own networked TV, meaning the festival offers its own bespoke on-site channel going out to bleary-eyed punters sat in their chalets taking stock after the battering the night before. Blessed with the same random madcap energy of public access TV of the 80s, recent years' programming has included a member of staff slowly spelling out the on-site WiFi password for about thirty minutes, and a man making an Airfix model of a galleon for over an hour to the sounds of DJ Airfix Twin. Bang Face is not for everyone. But even for those on the outside, you still have to marvel that something so deliciously unique exists.

From page 132, in order:
The Hard Crew get into it, 2008
Closing ceremony, 2019
Opening ceremony, 2016
Aphex Twin take the stage, 2012
Banners in the crowd, 2018

Rock en Seine

Born into a family of gardeners in 1613, André Le Nôtre would become France's pre-eminent designer of formal French gardens. He's best known for the grand and ordered symmetry of Versailles, as well as the gardens of Château de Saint-Cloud, which 400 years later provide the splendid and grand setting for one of France's most splendid and grand festivals.

Rock en Seine takes place amidst 450 acres and has become a legendary annual event. Held over the last weekend of August (not a bank holiday, as it is over the Channel in the UK, though popular with Brits and other Europeans for its comparatively low ticket prices), the name – a pun on the fact that the French word for 'stage' resembles the nearby Parisian waterway – is perennially misleading. Rock is just one of the many flavours that keep more than 100,000 fans flocking to it. Recent years have seen guitar mainstays such as The Cure joined by Aphex Twin and Jorja Smith as headliners. The setting of this multi-stage event in such an obviously splendid place definitely has a civilising effect on its crowds, who tread the fine line between respectful conduct and beer-chugging excess with – there's only one word for it – élan.

About the festival

Location • Paris, France

Started • 2003

Status • Still running

Notable headliners • Faith No More, Phoenix, Massive Attack, Placebo, Queens of the Stone Age

Famous for • Beautiful line-ups in a beautiful setting

Kindred spirits • Outside Lands, Benicàssim, Festival No.6, Eden Sessions, Bluedot, British Summer Time

Left:
The scenic Rock en Seine, 2015

Download

The world is riddled with ancient cliches about metal fans and metal bands alike. But Download Festival, possibly the most respected hard rock and metal festival there's ever been, shakes off all those lame preconceptions with an admittedly frantic nod of the head.

Download plays with its status as a formidable five-day assemblage of feral rock stars in ways that are, whisper it, actually rather cute. It fosters an amazing reputation for friendliness and politeness, perplexing if you take names like Slayer or Anthrax at face value. It has a lovable sense of community – just witness the forums and social pages that show how glad people are to find other Downloaders in their life. To make it seem even more like a minority sect in society, there are even Download Singles Dating pages, so you can make sure that you only ever date people who are, well, Downloady. Even cuter, VIP camping is known as RIP and though very, very pricey, offers clean toilets, hot showers, spa treatments plus – and we think this is a first for any festival we've ever seen – complimentary hair dryers and hair straighteners.

Donnington Park is a site already steeped in rock lore before Download began. Download is a continuation of the legacy of Monsters of Rock, an annual heavy rock festival that ran at the same site since 1980. The location has always been in the Midlands, a place synonymous with heavy metal since the late 60s, thanks to bands

About the festival

Location • Donnington Park, UK

Started • 2003

Status • Still running

Notable headliners • Black Sabbath, Slipknot, Metallica, Judas Priest, AC/DC

Famous for • Being the hard rock festival with the friendliest vibe imaginable

Kindred spirits • Rock in Rio, Rock am Ring, Hellfest, Wacken, Rock Werchter

From left, in order:
Corey Taylor of Slipknot onstage in 2019
The full festival experience at Donnington Park, 2016
Dressed to impress
Rocking out, 2019
Skindred onstage in 2019
Ozzy Osbourne headlines in 2018

like Black Sabbath, Judas Priest, Napalm Death and more. Its slightly 'trendy vicar'-esque name may not have dated especially well but it does reek of the year of its launch: 2003.

Seldom has a festival become so synonymous with mud as Download. It can be a hard-going festival, but its loyal punters overcome this for one simple reason: a love of music. Download treats its fans WELL in that regard. It's no surprise it engenders such loyalty – so few festivals take rock music as seriously and curate so damn well.

The list of acts to have graced the Download stage is pretty much definitive. Slipknot, Judas Priest, Black Sabbath, AC/DC, Alice Cooper, Def Leppard, System of a Down are just some, several having played many, many times over. Possibly the most over-the-top demand came in 2010 when AC/DC secured use of their own exclusive main stage (which included a full-scale steam train that weighed six tons, plus two sets of cannons). On the more modest extreme, Metallica played an unannounced, Glastonbury-esque secret afternoon set in 2003. Festival booker Andy Copping has only identified Foo Fighters, Pearl Jam and Van Halen as the acts that have eluded him over the years, as well as Led Zeppelin, to whom the festival made some big overtures in the past, but to no avail.

Beyond the headliners and the excellent undercard, a quirky buffet of non-musical entertainment exists at Download, from WWE appearances, stunt riding on a wall of death, medieval battle reenactments, funfairs and more. But at the beating heart of Download is a love of rock, and it's a love that bleeds from the organisers down to its loyal attendees, year after year.

Secret Garden Party

When you walk into a festival and the first thing you see is a naked man on a trampoline, you KNOW you're in a very blessed place indeed. Secret Garden Party, which ran for fourteen years, was the much-maligned and fairly misunderstood festival that somehow shifted the paradigm towards immersive boutique experiences and away from gawping at mega-bands.

It had the ironic tag line of 'This is a serious party' but plenty of cultural critics didn't see it that way, specifically accusing it of being a posh playground. SGP's co-founder, Freddie Fellowes, was the son of a lord and the young heir to the 6,000 acre estate that the festival sat on. But through the sheer force of its hedonistic reputation, it quickly transcended being a private-ish affair into becoming an essential part of British festival life. People who worked at festivals always made sure they cleared their calendars for SGP. So-hot-right-now bands and DJs would take vastly lower fees just as long as they could get a heaving guestlist for their posse. The largesse didn't stop there: I once hung out in a giant tent laid out in the campsite for techno legend Maya Jane Coles, which had sofas, CDJs and a full sound system just for her pals and entourage. Few festivals I've seen had such few barriers between the stage and the campsite.

About the festival

Location • Abbots Ripton, UK

Started • 2004

Status • Ended in 2017

Notable headliners • Metronomy, Grace Jones, Lily Allen, Jarvis Cocker

Famous for • Hedonism that eclipsed anything on the festival scene during the noughties and beyond

Kindred spirits • Standon Calling, Wilderness, Boomtown, Bestival, Meadows in the Mountains

Even though SGP had a main stage, and a decent hoard of big names have topped the bill over the years – Gorillaz, Jarvis Cocker, Blondie and Grace Jones (who many remember yelling off stage but still mic'd up 'I want to look like a fucking BANSHEE!'), SGP's real stars were always the crowds themselves. People genuinely saved their best looks, best drugs and best moves for that weekend. Its 'secret' schtick represented a desire to move away from big, behemoth festival experiences and really make it feel like a party. The result was that it gave ravers a thousand different places to play, each with their own characteristics.

The games arena (The Collisillium) was the heart of the festival during daytime – a gladiatorial ring made of steep hay bales that hosted madcap games such as naked mud wrestling or punters fighting on winches dressed as big Victorian babies. Then there was The Pagoda, a small jetty platform that hovered over the lake and once a year became possibly the finest dancefloor this writer has ever stepped onto. Waking up on Sunday morning, heading to The Pagoda and purging the demons of the night before with hours of sun-kissed dancing was a ritual enjoyed by many and forgotten by no one.

It was also a beautiful site set around a lake (where punters were allowed to swim) and played host to the early evening fireworks displays. Going through a Portaloo door revealed a vast and hidden field of sunflowers, grown to be in absolute dense splendour for the week of the festival. This was just one of several hundred beautiful experiences packed into a very bold and much-missed festival.

'When you walk into a festival and the first thing you see is a naked man on a trampoline, you KNOW you're in a very blessed place indeed.'

From page 144, in order:
Party mood on The Pagoda over the lake
Swimming and relaxing in the grounds, 2013
A boutique festival experience with plenty of places to play
An octopus attacks a sailing ship, 2014

Bestival

We mean this in the best possible way: Bestival was officially the silliest festival ever.

It sounds outlandish, but Bestival shifted the whole paradigm of what a festival should be. Before Bestival, festival-goers seldom looked, well, festive. If it was grey and repelled rain, it was fine to be worn for three days straight. What this much-loved UK festival did was put dressing-up at its heart. It inspired 50,000 people a year to get creative; suddenly, you and your spaceman costume were the real headliners, not the bands.

Bestival's general air of silliness was aided by the fact that it was held in a wonky theme park on the Isle of Wight. Most punters had to take a boozy ferry to reach the child-friendly delights of Robin Hill Country Park. It also helped that the organisers – DJ Rob da Bank and his wife, Josie – were hands-on hosts who were both super visible and also visibly loved having a good time. But it was Bestival's annual costume themes – such as Desert Island Disco, Summer of Love, Out of Space and Under the Sea – that proved the masterstroke.

Unlike Coachella-style festivals, dressing up at Bestival was about looking bonkers over beautiful. From its first modest incarnation in 2004, Saturday at Bestival was the day to rock your home-made look. A carnivalesque parade meandered over the site in the afternoon, with thousands of Bacofoil robots, harlequins, leopard onesies and Where's Wallys in attendance, many of

About the festival

Location • Isle of Wight, UK

Started • 2004

Status • On hiatus

Notable headliners • Amy Winehouse, Stevie Wonder, The xx, OutKast, Elton John

Famous for • Its army of fancy-dress warriors

Kindred spirits • Secret Garden Party, Bang Face Weekender, Lovebox

'... dressing up at Bestival was about looking bonkers over beautiful ...'

the costumes handmade by its smart, creative attendees. To remind you of how unserious it all was, the festival would fly over 90s TV fitness guru Mr Motivator from his home in Jamaica for the parade – mostly to stand on a flatbed truck and wave like a medieval king returned from exile.

Music-wise, Bestival managed to be both ruthlessly cutting-edge (flowing from the cachet of da Bank's own label and club night, Sunday Best), yet also a destination for some BIG household names: Elton, Stevie, Amy, Björk and Snoop were just some of the headliners over the festival's fourteen-year run.

But in truth, Bestival's whole ethos was to make the festival experience about more than just gawping up at headliners all weekend. In a similar vein to the immersive theatre scene that was booming around the late noughties, much of Bestival operated as series of nooks and crannies in which to encounter small delights up close. Punters could get lost in an endless supply of small, brightly coloured tents, a psychedelic wood, or even get 'married' in an inflatable church, administered by raucous Bristolians in dog collars. It also proudly hosted the world's biggest glitterball, and one year laid on a giant re-creation of Lionel Richie's head – which fans bowed down to all weekend, deity-like.

One year, as I stood on the rise of a hill, I saw a woman dressed as banana running and screaming for her life. A few seconds later came a human strawberry, similarly distressed. Then a pear. And finally, chasing them all, a man dressed as a food blender.

Though the festival ended in 2017, it left its mark. No longer would British festivals be a wasteland of burger vans, echoey rock bands and grey waterproofs.

From page 148, in order:
Festivalgoers embrace the Desert Island Disco theme, 2014
The main stage at Lulworth Estate, 2018
Crowds arriving at the grounds, 2014
The 2015 fancy dress parade, with the theme of the Summer of Love
An atmosphere of silliness and joyous fun

Flow Festival

Few modern festivals boast as much progressive flair as Finland's Flow Festival. Few do it better, in fact. This feted three-day affair takes place in Helsinki, at a former power plant called Suvilahti, whose steam turbine dates back to 1909 and whose skeleton gas holders form an iconic backdrop to this annual weekender.

Though it's obviously a hell of a trip for a festival to be set in a former power plant, what makes it such a cute proposition is that Flow has worked hard to become a carbon-neutral festival. All the electricity comes from recycled waste, while on-site food vendors are required to provide sustainable meal options, plus actual choices for vegetarians (not just falafel). Not that Flow lacks culinary grandeur – a Michelin-starred restaurant, Grön, has set up there previously, and there's also been a Lanson champagne bar. *Kippis!*

Just as distinctive as the post-industrial backdrop is Flow's Balloon stage, a 360-degree round platform that sees acts like Kamasi Washington and Pharaoh Sanders illuminated by an impossibly absorbing, giant colour-changing orb overhead. Possibly less distinctive are its headliners, which tend to follow the trend cycle of that year's big names on the festival circuit (previous acts include Kendrick Lamar, Alicia Keys, Iggy Pop, Nick Cave & The Bad Seeds and Björk). But on the flip side, in contrast to so many big events, the feeling of not being in thrall to the car to get home is palpable. Flow encourages

About the festival

Location • Helsinki, Finland

Started • 2004

Status • Still running

Notable headliners • Kanye West, Nick Cave & The Bad Seeds, Pet Shop Boys, Lana Del Rey

Famous for • Making an industrial site come alive with music and colour

Kindred spirits • Sónar, Melt, Tuska

'Flow has worked hard to become a carbon-neutral festival. All the electricity comes from recycled waste ...'

people to cycle to the festival (sadly there's no camping at Flow) by laying on an enormous amount of bike parking. Flow is one of the few European fests that doesn't feel overwhelmed by Brits abroad. It is generally uncelebrated outside of Finland and, this book aside, we kinda sorta hope it stays that way!

Lake of Stars

To anyone who has spent a lifetime enduring the rain-flecked, mud-strewn climate of most European festivals, the idea of a festival held on a beach is, quite frankly, dreamy. Lake of Stars, held at the Sunbird Nkopola Lodge on Lake Malawi, may be remote and a bit of a mission to reach, but it is well worth the journey to achieve the stuff of genuine dreams.

Like Nyege Nyege, Lake of Stars has European founders, which could ring problematic alarm bells. The festival was started by a student, Will Jameson, who visited Malawi back in 1998, then started a successful club night in Liverpool named Chibuku (after the Malawian beer Chibuku Shake Shake). Certainly the festival's aims are in step with the needs and wants of Malawi's cultural sector. Lake of Stars creates a much-needed platform for local artists, who don't often get the exposure they deserve. Hip hoppers like Suffix, or techno producer Drew Moyo, offer a contemporary take on Malawian music that rarely reaches the ears of those outside one of the poorest countries in Africa. That said, it's still able to draw in global stars who would rarely play a Western festival of such modest size. Since its debut in 2004, everyone from avant-garde Scottish hip hoppers Young Fathers, to bass-pumpers Major Lazer, to stadium-quakers Foals have played, as well as Beverley Knight, Bombay Bicycle Club and The Maccabees.

The simple, laid-back vibe, where drinks are affordable and beautiful sunrises

About the festival

Location • Chipoka, Malawi

Started • 2004

Status • Still running

Notable headliners • Foals, Young Fathers, Afrikan Boy

Famous for • Intimacy, Malawi-style

Kindred spirits • Nyege Nyege, WOMAD, Love International

'Lake of Stars creates a much-needed platform for local artists.'

reward anyone who can handle their drinks all night through, fosters a real community spirit among the 3,000-ish attendees – 60 per cent of whom are drawn from Malawi's cognoscenti. Add in movie screenings, poetry sessions and great food, and it's easy to see why Lake of Stars has become a destination for the world's more discerning festival heads.

Afropunk

There's Renaissance men, and then there's
James Spooner, founder of Afropunk. To
date, Spooner has been a tattoo artist,
label boss, zine-maker, DJ, promoter and
documentary-maker. As a young NYC-based
punk fan and a person of colour, he started
to wonder about his own place in punk – a
genre presented as almost indelibly white.
In 2003, he made a documentary called
Afro-Punk, which joined the dots for Black
punks everywhere and presented an
alternative to stereotypical notions of
Blackness in the process. It created such a
fresh, new energy, that having screened the
film 100 times across the country, he
decided the concept of Afro-punk badly
needed to exist in a physical space.

The original Afropunk shows didn't
belong exclusively to punk bands. 'You had
to have a Black singer, and you had to be
good by my standards,' stated Spooner
years later. 'That was it.' But where
Spooner's vision was to connect the many
disparate Black punks across the US, as the
event expanded, the purity hurtled out of
his dream and he eventually quit the festival
he'd christened.

The festival it subsequently mutated
into has its own energy, and despite the
acrimonious split with Cooper, what
remained has influenced the mainstream in
quite a profound way. Notions of Blackness
have altered significantly since the festival's
birth, and it's thanks to Afropunk that
Black artists are no longer pigeonholed as
either hip hop or R&B (as kept happening to

About the festival

Location • Atlanta, USA; Paris, France;
London, UK; Johannesburg, South Africa

Started • 2005

Status • Still running

Notable headliners • D'Angelo,
SZA, Lauryn Hill, Grace Jones

Famous for • Highlighting the other
Black experience

Kindred spirits • Harlem Cultural
Festival, WattStax, Afrochella

exemplary Afropunk favourite Santigold, to her despair). Janelle Monáe said during her 2018 performance: 'If it wasn't for Afropunk, I wouldn't have a career today.' Today, the mainstream world can deal with a tuxedo-wearing Black lesbian superstar who sounds a bit like Taylor Swift one minute and Prince the next – and for that alone, Afropunk gets our props.

'... he decided the concept of Afropunk badly needed to exist in a physical space.'

From page 160, in order:
Jojo Abot at Afropunk, 2017
Grace Jones held aloft during her set, 2015
Janelle Monáe onstage, 2016
Striking a pose in Atlanta, Georgia, 2018
Crowds gather at the front of the stage, 2019
Style on show, 2017 and 2018

Tomorrowland

With a wild and extravagant aesthetic, pitched somewhere between Liberace and Gianni Versace, Belgian dance music festival Tomorrowland is as outlandish as it is genuinely phenomenal.

The spectacle of Tomorrowland, as well as the fact it runs back-to-back weekends, is what gives it its edge. This is a festival that photographs extremely well and kinda knows it too. It has become synonymous for its big hulking stages, which improve magnificently on simply watching a DJ twiddling knobs. Some of the main stage creations reach over 120 metres high, take more than 40,000 hours to create and come festooned with performers and pyrotechnics that make the World Cup, the opening of the Olympics and NYE seem like it ain't no thang.

The festival began in 2005, and looking back at the visage of that first year is a lot like looking at pictures of an extravagant drag performer when they were square, timid and at uni. It's a shadow of its soon-to-be-self, even though for an event with just 9,000 attendees it was already punching above its weight in the glam department. Since 2009, each year's aesthetic has been given a theme (these include The Tree of Life, The Secret Kingdom of Melodia, The Elixir of Life, Amicorum Spectaculum, The Story of Planaxis); it reached a point when the stages got so big that they even contained full-sized archways under which people would walk to enter the main arena. They

About the festival

Location • Boom, Belgium

Started • 2005

Status • Still running

Notable headliners • Avicii, David Guetta, The Chainsmokers, Martin Garrix, Armin van Buuren

Famous for • Some of the most lavish stages ever!

Kindred spirits • Electric Daisy Carnival, Creamfields, Vh1 Supersonic, ZoukOut

'Some of the main stage creations reach over 120 metres high, take more than 40,000 hours to create ...'

are not merely backdrops for the DJ – they *are* the show.

The adult playground vibe is carried on over an astonishing number of stages – often as many as eighteen – which offer everything from relative intimacy to stadia-sized throngs, all crucially decked and designed in the most ornate and extravagent fashion. Some, like the Freedom stage, are clad almost entirely in LED displays, while others such as the Rave Cave are simply that – small boltholes for an experience much, MUCH more akin to dance music's intimate clubbing roots. There's an irony there though, as spectacle-heavy productions like Tomorrowland buoyed the rise of global rave sounds such as EDM (David Guetta, Carl Cox, Afrojack, Armin van Buuren, Eric Prydz, Martin Garrix) more than anything, and led to the rise of DJs playing pre-mixed sets only so they could be timed to pyrotechnics and fireworks like a Vegas show.

The extravagance doesn't end with the stage design. VIP access can include viewing platforms next to the main stage offering jacuzzis, swimsuits and massage chairs. Another stage has a swimming pool built next to it, while toilets carry deodorant in them (win!). There's also a daily newspaper, and Michelin-starred chefs create Michelin-starred meals for Michelin-starred prices, too.

As an on-the-ground experience, Tomorrowland is interestingly aware of nationality. Organisers state that ticket buyers come from over 200 different countries (a factor that explains why, like Glastonbury, each year's event sells out in a matter of minutes); it takes over a whole terminal at Brussels Airport. It's also apparent from the crowd, who frequently display their national flag in their clothing or bag as a conversation starter. It all lends to the feeling that if EDM is truly the music of the globe, then Tomorrowland is its United Nations.

From page 166, in order:
The extravagant stage, featuring giant replicas of vintage book jackets, 2019
Fireworks at the main stage during DJ Tiësto's set, 2019
De Schorre, the provincial recreation area in Boom, Belgium, that hosts the festival
Bewinged revellers, 2019
The extraordinary forest design, 2016

Way Out West

For most weekends of the Swedish summer, two of the biggest draws of Slottsskogen Park in Gothenburg would be a pair of splendid and iconically native Swedish animals: the Gute sheep and the Gotland pony. Yet the park (influenced in design by London's Hyde Park) and its admittedly awesome petting zoo play second fiddle on the second weekend of August – as four stages, a heaving sack of big-name acts and a delightful crowd take over the scenically lush and lake-pocked site.

Like that other Scandi fest Øya (and in fact like many festivals founded in the 2010s generally), WOW is deeply aware of its ecological impact. This in turn led to the festival deciding in 2012 to go with an exclusively vegetarian set of food vendors. Though this would subsequently please 2016 headliner Morrissey, it created a hilarious tabloid scandal at the time. So much so that Swedish newspaper *GT* riled the festivals' organisers by turning up and handing out free sausages and meatballs to attendees on its first meat-free year. Meat is still out, and also prohibitions around drinking mean that boozing at certain stages is forbidden, but it hardly dampens the mood. Like many Scandinavian festivals, there's a real caché to WOW's line-ups, and that's what makes the festival's four stages so alluring. From 2007's debut year bagging Kanye and Erykah Badu, to recent years seeing The Strokes, The Cure, Cardi B and PJ Harvey all straddling the upper orders, WOW is not

About the festival

Location • Gothenburg, Sweden

Started • 2007

Status • Still running

Notable headliners • The Strokes, Cardi B, Pet Shop Boys, Stormzy, Frank Ocean

Famous for • Surely the finest line-ups in all Scandinavia?

Kindred spirits • We Love Green, Vieilles Charrues Festival, Benicàssim, Oxegen, Parklife,

From left, in order:
Scenic Slottsskogen Park, which plays host to the festival
Line-up posters, 2017 and 2008
Cruising on a flamingo inflatable, 2017
Posing with the Way Out West sign, 2013
Fans watch Håkan Hellström perform, 2013

an erroneous acronym when it comes to star appeal. Visitors in 2019 made much of the spectacle of a Doritos cannon firing multiple packets of crisps into the air – causing as much of a mud-soaked frenzy as Stormzy's mosh pit that same year – but commercial distractions from the stage are thankfully rare.

Though there's no camping at Way Out West, attendees can still see the night through in the city centre, where venues take part in Stay Out West, which sees Gothenburg throw itself open to festival-goers for after-hours gigs and clubs. A hella civilised way to wind down, if ever we've seen one.

'Visitors in 2019 made much of the spectacle of a Doritos cannon firing multiple packets of crisps into the air ...'

Kappa FuturFestival

One of Italy's great exports to the artistic world was Futurism – the movement that roundly dishonoured tradition and championed the beauty of the new at the turn of the twentieth century. It's fitting that a movement that feted speed, youth and technology would play a small part in launching techno-loving Turin festival, Kappa FuturFestival.

This two-dayer initially began as a one-off: it was conceived as part of the celebrations for a century of Futurist thinking. But KFF – or to give it its formal title, The Torino Summer Music Festival – has since galloped ahead with its own aesthetic. While organisers estimate that around 25 per cent of attendees are from abroad, KFF is a demonstrably Italian affair. From 2012, the renamed event was sponsored by the iconically logo'd Kappa sportswear brand, whose perma-youthful image belies the fact that it's a company that's existed for over 100 years. Kappa FuturFestival is legitimately a young affair though, and seems to mine Turin's reserves of lean, good-looking dance music fans, all basking in the guaranteed scorch of the city in July.

It's held annually at Parco Dora – a vast modern scheme that converted an area of Turin's industrial wasteland into pleasurable open space, incorporating the iconic pillars

About the festival

Location • Turin, Italy

Started • 2009

Status • Still running

Notable headliners • Solomun, Nina Kraviz, Marco Carola, Richie Hawtin

Famous for • Techno, techno and more techno

Kindred spirits • Junction 2, Time Warp, Movement Electronic

'What began as a celebration of Futurists has become a celebration of names from techno's top table ...'

From page 174, in order:
Huge crowds gather, 2019
The almost camouflaged Dora stage, 2019
Amelie Lens, triumphantly waving the Italian flag, 2019
Carl Cox taking a selfie with the crowd, 2019
Nina Kraviz performing, 2019

and smokestacks of the past, which are a huge part of KFF's landscaping and look. What began as a celebration of Futurists such as Marinetti, Carrà, Balla and Palazzeschi has become a celebration of names from techno's top table: Cox, Hawtin, Villalobos, Kraviz and Prydz have all played across Kappa FuturFestival's four stages.

Strawberry Fields

I once asked globe-trotting DJ hero The Blessed Madonna what was the worst thing she'd ever seen at a festival. She replied with deadly succinctness: 'psy-trance'.

It's fair to say that psychedelic trance often brings out the worst in people. For some reason, people who are otherwise kind, respectful and tolerant become as poisonous as a puff adder when confronted with tie-dye, dreads and the mere hint of fire poi. Yet though the Australian Strawberry Fields started off as an 800-capacity psy-trance festival in 2009, it has leapfrogged over its – how shall we say – culturally divisive roots and come to be the envy of festivals around the world for its remoteness and removal from the normal world.

Located a few hours from Melbourne, on the border between Melbourne and Sydney and flanked by the majestic Murray River, this Bush Doof (slang for alternative raves held in the Australian countryside, far from cities) has grown and grown. In fact, Strawberry Fields has, strictly speaking, transcended the Doof tag, given the quite stunning (and very trendy) line-ups it attracts to its decadent parties. In that sense, the festival has hurtled past its psy-trance roots – but it's important to remember that line-ups aren't everything. The festival's freedom, its bohemian,

About the festival

Location • Melbourne, Australia

Started • 2009

Status • Still running

Notable headliners • Helena Hauff, Juan Atkins, Nightmares on Wax, CC:Disco!

Famous for • Being the world's best known 'bush doof'

Kindred spirits • Boomtown, Glade, Shambala

From left, in order:
Friends dancing, 2019
Revellers enjoying the festival within the colourfully designed structure, 2019
People gather to relax beside the lake, 2019
The festival, illuminated at night
Crowds gather for a DJ set, 2019

'It has become a genuinely awe-inspiring, free-wheeling affair, and thus attracts big-name DJs.'

While stages are modest in size, they're often big in vibe. And none more so than the Beach stage, which naturally helps scorched ravers cool and soothe just a little from the – it has to be said – omnipresent dust. The real headliner every year, though, is the phalanx of enormous red gum trees that define the landscape of this spectacular and secluded affair.

no-fucks-given style sense and its young adherents are all products of its roots and origins. It has become a genuinely awe-inspiring, free-wheeling affair, and thus attracts big-name DJs who can rise to such a crowd: Honey Dijon, Helena Hauff, Derrick May, Andrew Weatherall and Leftfield, to name just a few.

Dimensions

Built at the tail-end of the nineteenth century by the Austro-Hungarian empire to protect and defend the important port city of Pula, Fort Punta Christo is vast.

Abandoned and derelict at the start of the early 2000s, its rebirth began when a group of enthusiastic friends discovered the inaccessible site and embarked on a labour of love, slowly clearing fallen trees and overgrown shrubs to open it up (along with its views of the coast). They formed groups to take over administration of the fort, and a fundraising bar turned into a party, which turned into a bigger party, and then a festival called Seasplash. Two British festivals, Outlook and Dimensions, subsequently brought the site to life.

Dimensions' programming made the site come alive. As if to illustrate the casual grandeur of the experience, the festival kicks off with an opening concert in a vast Roman amphitheatre in Pula, which dates back to 120 BCE. Little Dragon, Caribou, Massive Attack, Anderson .Paak, Nils Frahm and Kraftwerk have all had the honour of playing there.

But for the festival's 7,000 punters, many more seemingly improbable spaces exist. Most notable is The Moat – literally in a deep empty moat ensconced in tall stone walls to form a raver cocoon. Once daylight comes, camping or hotels take the burden of sweaty bodies – but only for a bit, as the next day beach parties fill with finely curated, sun-kissed sounds to slowly invigorate the crowd.

About the festival

Location • Tisno, Croatia

Started • 2011

Status • Still running

Notable headliners • Kraftwerk, Warpaint, Caribou, George Clinton, Anderson .Paak, Bonobo

Famous for • The glory days when it occurred around a derelict fort

Kindred spirits • Outlook, Melt, Hideout, Electric Elephant, Love International, Exit

For the more hardy and gung-ho, Dimensions, as with all other Croatian festivals, offers the chance of hopping on a daytime party boat. On the right day, they really are a highlight of the summer.

Picking one of the many excellent Croatian festivals based either at Pula or at the Garden Tisno is hard. But Dimensions always has great line-ups, buzzy and friendly yet mature crowds (55 per cent British and another 45 per cent from a host of countries), and the ability to make paradise really come alive.

Left:
The Stables stage at night

Dekmantel

If the BBC's lavish coverage of Glastonbury helped make the festival a global institution, then a similar relationship might help explain the justified hype for Dutch dance music festival Dekmantel.

Boiler Room, the London-based music-streaming experts, truly put Dekmantel on the map, thanks to the video broadcasts from their own tunnel-shaped stage at Amsterdamse Bos (the city park that hosts the annual festival). The sight of ravers exploding with joy under its curved roof is an emblematic sight in modern dance music. Yet there's so much more to Dek than a cheeky rave video can convey.

Dekmantel (also a record label) traditionally kicks off in a high-brow-and-proud way, at the Muziekgebouw aan 't IJ, a majestic riverside concert hall that gives way to unconventional legends of electronic music: Manuel Göttsching, Autechre and Tangerine Dream have all occupied this coveted pre-weekend slot.

The main festival takes place in the park and is just the most splendid coming together of acts and fans imaginable. Given that the majority of Dekmantel's bookings are deck-wrangling DJs, it does have certain limitations. For example, it's mostly held in daytime (with an 11pm curfew, but with afterparties in clubs across Amsterdam), and the sunny vibe means the traditional razzle-dazzle of a light show isn't an option. Yet despite this, Dekmantel goes beyond, to create a vibe that is both unique and conducive to dancing.

About the festival

Location • Amsterdam, Netherlands

Started • 2013

Status • Still running

Notable headliners • Joy Orbison, Tangerine Dream, Jamie xx, Lena Willikens, Helena Hauff

Famous for • Being your favourite DJ's favourite festival

Kindred spirits • Sónar, Movement Electronic, Unsound, Houghton

The Greenhouse stage is a divine space boasting tall palms and bamboos in a predictably steamy and glass-roofed hangar. On the flip side, the enormous wall of audacious digital colour that cradles the main stage is yet another iconic vision in global raving. When populated by the pantheon of DJs selected by Dekmantel every year, these stages magically become some of the most coveted in the world.

Left:
The majestic Muziekgebouw aan 't IJ concert hall kick-starts the festival

Nyege Nyege

'An uncontrollable urge to move, shake or dance'. That's just one definition of the Lugandan term 'nyege nyege'. Another is along the lines of 'horny horny'. Both phrases have been served well by its namesake festival, which has taken place annually near the city of Jinja in Uganda since 2015.

On the one hand, it's just a straight-up amazing party in a beautiful setting. Occupying a never-officially-opened holiday resort called Nile Discovery Centre, a short ride from the city, NN takes places amidst sun-bathed clearings in a lush tropical forest. It's pretty hard to dislike, even before you take into account the verdant campsites and the chance to bathe in the Nile whenever you fancy.

Energy levels are HIGH. This isn't a festival for chin-strokers and head-nodders; it's a properly engaged rave where the low stages and intimate vibe really put the crowd in the limelight. The festival does well, drawing in punters from Europe, and has a global reputation via streams on platforms like Boiler Room, but obviously the crowd is mostly local.

A party is a party, but what sets Nyege Nyege apart is its devotion to the avant-garde and the bleeding edge of experimental music. While you will definitely hear mainstream EDM and afrobeats bangers whizz by in crowd-pleasing sets, Nyege Nyege has become famed as a hub for hype African electronic music. Styles like kwaito, balani, kuduro and footwork are often

About the festival

Location • Jinja, Uganda

Started • 2013

Status • Still running

Notable headliners • Kampire, Nilotica Drum Ensemble, Josey Rebelle, Shyboi

Famous for • High spirits that surpass almost any other fest on Earth

Kindred spirits • Dekmantel, Afrochella, Oppikoppi, Afro Nation

featured, as part of a conscious bookings policy to collate the best of the modern sounds of the African diaspora. In recent years, this has ranged from the relentless electro percussion of Kampala's Nihiloxica, the otherworldly palpitations of Jlin, or the stomping art-rave of Juliana Huxtable.

Nyege Nyege is a hard festival to make work. Apparently even the basics – from Portaloos to CDJs – are extremely hard to source. But for the sheer exuberance alone, it's worth all the effort.

The Crave

Dutch festival The Crave is certainly one of the more niche, under-the-radar events mentioned in this book. But its hallowed reputation and word-of-mouth buzz has given it a profile few festivals can rival.

Set away from the powerhouse of dance music that is Amsterdam, The Crave reps the coastal city of The Hague hard. It also fosters a loyal crowd that goes hard, too. Driven by lashings of techno of all denominations, it's an annual, cutely-sized, 5,000-capacity affair, which takes place in the stunningly picturesque Zuiderpark. Set in woodland and bordered by a tranquil lake, getting around The Crave's four stages is a fun frolic through a pleasingly natural environment. As night descends, trippy artful projections come into their own and only add to the sense of other-worldliness. Not that the daytime lacks oddities: take the random old-school exercise bikes, just sitting there waiting for a raver to park their bum and maybe chance a little pedal.

Global dance music website Resident Advisor nailed it by calling The Crave 'more like a free party than a ticketed festival'. While the event runs normal one-day festival hours (midday-ish until midnight-ish), it's the rave-hardened yet impossibly friendly crowds that elevate the whole day into something beyond. Where most festivals have a contingent of flaky wallflowers, seemingly everyone at The Crave treats it as a life source. It's no wonder that the lucky selectors who have been gifted the very real privilege to play often cite their sets at The Crave as the highlight of their summer.

About the festival

Location • The Hague, Netherlands

Started • 2014

Status • Still running

Notable headliners • Nina Kraviz, Tom Trago, Egyptian Lover, Aurora Halal

Famous for • Being one of the most joyous days imaginable for underground dance fans

Kindred spirits • Dekmantel, Sónar, AVA Festival, Unsound, Houghton

Huge pride of place is given to local artists, yet it is still a destination for the world's finest house, electro and techno dream-weavers. From the harsh and fast beats of Detroit's DJ Stingray, to the hypnotic pulse of London's Hessle Audio crew, to originators such as Egyptian Lover, it's easy to see why DJs and dancers rave about The Crave.

Left:
The festival takes place at the stunningly picturesque Zuiderpark

Magnetic Fields

Few events have put India's bubbly underground music scene on the map as much as Magnetic Fields: a stunningly decadent-yet-actually-cool event held annually in a quiet town in Rajasthan.

The first, most obvious, asset of this three-day festival is its ridiculous location. Magnetic Fields takes place in no less than a genuine palace. Many British festivals, from Knebworth to Camp Bestival, have taken place in the shadow of grand heritage buildings, but few actually let you inside. Built in the seventeenth century, and around six hours from Delhi, the former residence of courtly nobleman The Thakur of Alsisar is an absurdly plush pile for a family and festival alike.

In among the many spaces the palace has to offer, such as its central courtyard, that houses the main stage, are ten stages which tend to host small but dedicated crowds who vibe the intimacy and communal spirit – similar to most small dancefloors, in fact. There are also stages set up in the nearby desert, among the camping village. Accommodation combines some chi-chi on-site options – a mix of classic and Bedouin tents – as well as paid-for homestays in the local area (thankfully it's one of those festivals that lets you come and go as you please, rather than tries to confine you and bleed every

About the festival

Location • Rajasthan, India

Started • 2014

Status • Still running

Notable headliners • Shanti Celeste, Joy Orbison, Charanjit Singh, Midland, Objekt

Famous for • Its genuinely luxurious setting

Kindred spirits • Wilderness, Bahidorá, Oasis Festival

last dollar, pound and rupee out of you).
Yoga, wellness and Ayurvedic massage are
on offer in the Magic Sanctuary, to keep the
endorphins rushing.

What has made Magnetic Fields such an
important event, though, is its weight of
homegrown talent. India's reggae selectors,
techno producers and dubstep makers
rarely penetrate the European and American
trend bubble, but Magnetic Fields gives a
much-needed platform to India's coolest.
From the roots sound system attitude
of Begum X and Delhi Sultanate, to the
renegade techno of Arjun Vagale, to drummer
and activist Madame Gandhi, Magnetic
Fields combines India's regal past with its
white-hot underground present.

From page 192, in order:
Seated festival-goers take in a performance, 2015
Austrian act HVOB onstage, 2015

Secret Solstice

Surely no other festival uses the natural assets of its surroundings better than Iceland's Secret Solstice. Ever fancied a geothermic pool party? Such hot lake lols can be yours, with a big-name DJ playing pool-side, of course. How about a rave in a cave? SS offers side gigs in an actual glacier, but with a two-drink maximum, lest anyone get too drunk to behave appropriately in the relatively perilous surroundings. What about a gig in a lava tunnel? Created 5,200 years ago by a volcanic eruption, the festival uses the high-ceilinged Raufarhólshellir lava tunnels for intimate gigs.

If all of this sounds novel and bonkers in equal measure, wait for the real coup de grace: Secret Solstice takes place in permanent light, over its entire seventy-two hours. Always held in June, during the period known across the Arctic Circle as Midnight Sun, the darkest it gets is a trippy, colourful, darkish hue at midnight, as the sun reaches the horizon before rebounding up again. It gives the festival – held amidst the hot springs of the Laugardalur neighbourhood of Reykjavik – an insane energy. Factor in Secret Solstice's perennially young crowd (perhaps inevitable with a fest of such insane duration), and a bookings policy that's always nicely sync'd with the zeitgeist (previous acts include anyone from Patti Smith to Lil Pump), and you have a truly unique and epically Icelandic take on the traditional music festival.

About the festival

Location • Reykjavik, Iceland

Started • 2014

Status • Still running

Notable headliners • Radiohead, Slayer, Foo Fighters, Deftones, Of Monsters and Men

Famous for • Being held under almost constant daylight

Kindred spirits • Eurockéennes, Pukkelpop, Outside Lands

From left, in order:
Party atmosphere at the Secret Lagoon, 2016
The cavernous Lava Tunnel

Oasis Festival

Wellness and relaxation are the biggest hooks that draw visitors to Oasis Festival in Morocco. In many ways it's the same for the country itself, which has a long association with making people say 'ahhhhhhhh' via its famed spas and hammams. Yoga amidst palm trees, a pool by the main stage, a champagne bar, bohemian Bedouin hangouts … yes, it's an actual Instagram paradise, but there's way more to it than that.

Oasis is a relatively new addition to the North African festival scene. It began in 2015 as a festival-cum-holiday experience, offering both the chance of a September break in the great city of Marrakech and a sublime-yet-subtle grown-up festival experience with all the sonic trimmings. Oasis always bags a brilliant cast of contemporary names – you'd imagine aided a little bit by its ability to offer artists a stay at a lush resort close to the Atlas Mountains. Techno kings such as Carl Cox and Sasha, Balearic monster DJ Harvey, plus other loved spinners, such as The Blessed Madonna, Octo Octa, Moodymann and Theo Parrish have all joined the luxurious scene in the past.

Festival founder Marjana Jaidi sees Oasis as a vehicle for promoting a more progressive, forward-thinking perception of Morocco. It sees a fifty-fifty-ish split between local attendees and foreign guests,

About the festival

Location • Marrakech, Morocco

Started • 2015

Status • Still running

Notable headliners • The Blessed Madonna, Nicolas Jaar, Solomun, Richie Hawtin, Maceo Plex

Famous for • Absolute, total bliss

Kindred spirits • Meadows in the Mountains, Magnetic Fields, Bahidorá

and reps the nation's culture with a vibrant pop-up from the Musée d'Art Contemporain Africain Al Maaden (MACAAL), as well as performances from Moroccan ensembles of Ahwash performers.

When asked about the Oasis spirit, Moroccan DJ hero Amine K said: 'Electronic music has always been about having an open mind and accepting everybody the way they are, no matter the nationality, the ethnicity, the religion or the sexual orientation. Morocco has had this culture for decades.' Viewing dance music through the Moroccan gaze is just one joyful aspect of this very joyful festival.

Mighty Hoopla

Being gay at a music festival has historically been a slightly sad, slightly grim prospect. The lazy straightness of rock and its command of the scene offered very little sparkle, shine or solidarity. Queer visibility in programming was almost non-existent, and for LGBT+ attendees, festivals failed to offer a space to be gay, let alone a whole event where being straight was the exception rather than the rule.

Yet there is a recent shining light. Few have done it bigger, better or gayer than London's Mighty Hoopla.

As a new wave of LGBT+ activism in the late 2010s came to reinvigorate the global arts and culture scene, so it would seem inevitable that a delightful one-day gay-oriented festival would burst forth like paper from a confetti cannon. In reality, though, Mighty Hoopla was the climax of a decade-long resurgence in camp, left-field and DIY nightlife, which evangelised a progressive idea of gender non-conformity, a shameless love of pop and a really healthy sense of silliness that only Britain's capital could concoct. All this coalesced at Sink The Pink – the game-changing drag club from which Hoopla was born, which began at a former working men's club in London's East End.

Hoopla's first London outing in 2017 was a revelation. Held in the always

About the festival

Location • London, UK

Started • 2016

Status • Still running

Notable headliners • Chaka Khan, TLC, Lily Allen, Years & Years

Famous for • Hoisting a big, fabulous rainbow flag above the festival scene

Kindred spirits • SuncéBeat, Way Out West, Lovebox, Milkshake, Yo! Sissy, Wigstock, Big Gay Out

From left, in order:
Festival-goers strike a pose
Sink The Pink perform, 2018
Vibrant colours are a hallmark of the festival
Kate Nash performing in 2019
Dancers performing
Working the camera

accommodating Victoria Park, it offered an explosion of open-air colour and queerness that hadn't been seen in a generation. Here was a festival space in which being gay wasn't a compromise, it was the norm. It was also an unashamed pop extravaganza, as much a revolution for not hearing shredding rock guitars or soulless techno blasting across a multi-stage site. While All Saints, Will Young and Years & Years all played, the novelties were just as prominent as the headliners. A tent hosting a mass Spice Girls singalong looked at one point like it might actually explode.

Its move a year later to the more conservative Brockwell Park went just as smoothly, save for local residents' dogs amusingly finding dildos in the bushes once TLC, Lily Allen and Melanie C (flanked by drag versions of her former bandmates) had left the stage. It took just a couple of years, but a dyed-in-the-wool gay music festival quickly became the new normal and part of the festival furniture, albeit decades and decades overdue.

Mad Cool

A line-up as good as anything else out there, but with glorious sizzling Spanish sun and mud-repelling Astroturf everywhere, to prevent you writhing around in filth all weekend – that's the angle with Mad Cool, which has been a jewel in the crown of the Iberian festival scene since it began in 2016.

Originally held in the Caja Mágica in 2016 and 2017, Mad Cool shifted to open-air space Valdebebas in 2018. Unlike many successful festivals, Mad Cool switched its model in 2019 to have a smaller capacity over more days (four instead of three) in a bid to tackle overcrowding at various stages. As with many southern European fests, there's no camping, so guests stay in rented accommodation across the 'Mad' part of 'Mad Cool'; the festival itself charmingly attributes it all to the city of Madrid, stating, 'We have become what we are in such a short time thanks to the public and the people of Madrid ... that energy, that love for music and for culture. Mad Cool is its reflection.'

The action doesn't begin until around 6pm-ish, leaving space in the daytime for sun, sightseeing, shopping and, most importantly, sleep, before the bands kick off at this typically more-boozy-than-hedonistically-druggy festival. Standard European festival prices will get you access to a top-tier bill that has included Billie Eilish, Taylor Swift, The Killers, Iggy Pop and The Cure, plus DJs such as Four Tet, Diplo and Modeselektor playing The Loop tent.

About the festival

Location • Madrid, Spain

Started • 2016

Status • Still running

Notable headliners • Pearl Jam, The National, Green Day, Radiohead

Famous for • Possibly being the perfect city festival

Kindred spirits • Primavera, Rock en Seine, All Points East, Wireless

Even by modern festival standards, the edible offerings at Mad Cool are affordable, varied and delicious in equal measure. Anyone for tapas, Mexican snacks, calamari sandwiches and, as the site claims, 'an array of meats with certified designations of origin'? I know I am. There's also an on site market and a monster Ferris wheel offering views of the whole of Madrid.

For many, Mad Cool occupies the space of being an incredible accessory to a perfect Spanish holiday. What it maybe lacks in terms of originality and otherness, it more than makes up for in splendour and sun.

From page 210, in order:
Crowds wander past giant structures and the big wheel
Festival-goers wearing extravagant costumes
People relaxing in front of the stage, 2016
Lauryn Hill, 2019
Dua Lipa performing in 2018
Rosalía takes to the stage, 2019

Index

Index of festivals by country

Index of festivals by month

Index of festivals by musical genre

Jazz • Bonnaroo (35; 81); Jazzablanca (43); Love Supreme Festival (43); Meltdown (119); Montreal International Jazz Festival (11); Montreux Jazz Festival (11-3; 43); New Orleans Jazz & Heritage Festival (11; 43); Newport Jazz Festival (11); North Sea Jazz Festival (11; 43)

Metal • Afropunk (161-5); Big Day Out (65; 77-9; 115); Download (39; 49; 53; 99; 139-143); Hellfest (49; 99; 139); Monsters of Rock (53); Reading (27; 35; 39-41; 65; 77); Rock am Ring (49-51; 53; 139); Rock in Rio (49; 53; 139); Sonisphere (49; 53); Tuska (99-101; 153); Wacken (49; 139)

Pop • Benicàssim (81; 109; 137; 171); Big Gay Out (205); Blissfields (115); Clockenflap (77); Coachella (69; 109-113); Eden Sessions (137); Eurockéennes (197); Flow Festival (95; 153-5); Glastonbury (15; 21; 27-33; 39; 45; 87; 109); Isle of Wight Festival (15-9; 21; 27); Latitude (115); Lovebox (77; 127-9; 149; 205); Mad Cool (211-3); Mighty Hoopla (127; 205-9); Oppikoppi (187); Outside Lands (137; 197); Rock in Rio (49; 53; 139); T in the Park (77); Tuska (99-101; 153); Way Out West (35; 171-3; 205)

Psychedelic Rock • Altamont Free Concert (21); Woodstock (15; 21-5; 27; 65)

Punk • Download (39; 49; 53; 99; 139-143); Hellfest (49; 99; 139); Reading (27; 35; 39-41; 65; 77)

R&B • Afro Nation (187); KISSTORY (103); Lovebox (77; 127-9; 149; 205); Montreux Jazz Festival (11-3; 43); North Sea Jazz Festival (11; 43); Wireless (39; 109; 127; 211)

Rave • AfrikaBurn (55; 123-5); All Tomorrow's Parties (133); Arcadia (95); AVA Festival (85; 191); Bang Face Weekender (133-5; 149); Bestival (81; 145; 149-151); Bloc Weekend (133); Boomtown (27; 145; 179); Burning Man (55-9; 73; 95; 123); Creamfields (103; 167); Electric Daisy Carnival (69-71; 167);

Dimensions (183); Global Gathering (103); Hideout (73; 183); Kappa FuturFestival (175-7); Labyrinth Festival (85); Love International (157; 183); Meadows in the Mountains (87; 145; 199); Melt (81; 95-7; 153; 183); Midburn (55); Nowhere (55); Secret Garden Party (73; 145-7; 149); Nuits Sonores (105; 131); Outlook (183); Parklife (127; 171); Sónar (85; 119; 131; 153; 185; 191); Strawberry Fields (179-181); Tomorrowland (167-9); Tribal Gathering (103)

Rock • Afropunk (161-5); Altamont Free Concert (21); Big Day Out (65; 77-9; 115); Blissfields (115); British Summer Time (127; 137); Coachella (69; 109-113); Download (39; 49; 53; 99; 139-143); Eden Sessions (137); Flow Festival (95; 153-5); Fuji Rock (87-9); Girls Just Wanna Weekend (91); Glastonbury (15; 21; 27-33; 39; 45; 87; 109); Hellfest (49; 99; 139); Isle of Wight Festival (15-9; 21; 27); Lollapalooza (65-7; 109); Mad Cool (211-3); Monsters of Rock (53); Monterey Pop Festival (15; 21); Open'er (81); Outside Lands (137; 197); Oxegen (171); Pukkelpop (87; 197); Reading (27; 35; 39-41; 65; 77); Rock am Ring (49-51; 53; 139); Rock en Seine (137); Rock in Rio (49; 53; 139); Rock Werchter (53; 99; 139); Roskilde (35-7); Secret Solstice (197); Sonisphere (49; 53); Summer Sonic (39); Sziget (81-3); T in the Park (77); Tuska (99-101; 153); Vh1 Supersonic (69; 167); Way Out West (35; 171-3; 205); Wacken (49; 139); Woodstock (15; 21-5; 27; 65)

Soul • Harlem Cultural Festival (161); Love Supreme Festival (43); Lovebox (77; 127-9; 149; 205); Montreux Jazz Festival (11-3; 43); North Sea Jazz Festival (11; 43); Oppikoppi (187); Wattstax (161)

Techno • Amsterdam Dance Event (85); Arcadia (95); AVA Festival (85; 191); Bestival (81; 145; 149-151); Bloc Weekend (133); Burning Man (55-9; 73; 95; 123); Creamfields (103; 167); Dekmantel (85; 131; 185; 187; 191); Dimensions (183); Generation Move (63); Glade (179); Global

Gathering (103); Hideout (73; 183); Houghton (185; 191); Junction 2 (175); Kappa FuturFestival (175-7); KaZantip (73-5); Labyrinth Festival (85); Lake Parade (63); Lost & Found (73); Love International (157; 183); Love Parade (61-3); Meadows in the Mountains (87; 145; 199); Melt (81; 95-7; 153; 183); Movement Electronic (175; 185); Nuits Sonores (105; 131); Nyege Nyege (157; 187-9); Oasis Festival (193; 199-203); Outlook (183); Parklife (127; 171); Sónar (85; 119; 131; 153; 185; 191); Strawberry Fields (179-181); The Crave (191); Time Warp (85; 175); Tribal Gathering (103); Union Move (63); Unsound (185; 191); Vision Parade (63); Yo! Sissay (205)

World • Oslo World (45); Rainforest World Music Festival (45); Shambala (179); WOMAD (45-7; 87; 157)

Acknowledgements

My life changed in 2008 when I drove a vehicle
full of giant Scrabble tiles to a festival,
in exchange for a free ticket and the chance
to hang out with some cool kids hosting a
tent. They badly needed DJs, so I offered to
play with whatever random car CDs I had.
Two hours later, with the tent miraculously
packed, sweaty and gurning, I only had one
song left: 'Girl From Mars' by Ash. It bombed,
spectacularly, yet that weekend opened
my eyes to fun – finally – and gifted me the
finest friends imaginable. Everlasting
gratitude to Rob Wilson, endless love to
everyone involved with Lost & Found and
here's to the future, Egg crew.

For propping me up through 'hell year',
I'm deeply indebted to Bonnie Jones, Kim
Taylor Bennett, Adam Redmore, Andy
Kobelinsky, Pops, Tim Barnsdall and Clayton
Wright. For a lifetime of perfect unflinching
love, thank you to my mother, Guity.

I'm hugely grateful to Nicki Davis and
Joe Hallsworth at Quarto for the opportunity,
to Kyle MacNeill for the research and to
Kate Hutchinson for the constant journalistic
support and kinship.

Thank you to *Time Out* for generally
leaving me alone to cover festivals ad nauseam.
Thanks also to all the many, many festival pros
who helped me out with this book, filling in
blanks and offering mud-flecked perspectives.
My VIP wristband is your VIP wristband.

Clarence and Charlotte, you are my
eternal headliners. I love you.

Picture Credits

The publishers would like to thank the festivals, picture libraries and photographers for their kind permission to reproduce the works featured in this book. Every effort has been made to trace all copyright holders but if any have been inadvertently overlooked, the publishers would be pleased to make the necessary arrangements at the first opportunity.

2 Evening Standard/Stringer/Getty 6t Universal Images Group/ Getty 6b Matt Cardy/Stringer/Getty 8–9 Sandor Csudai 10 Keystone Press/Alamy 11 Richard Coulstock/Alamy 12 ullstein bild Dtl./Getty 13 Keystone Press/Alamy 14 MIKE WALKER/Alamy 17 Robert Young/Mirrorpix/Getty 18t Daily Mirror/Mirrorpix/ Mirrorpix via Getty 18b Rolls Press/Popperfoto/Getty 19t Simon Robinson/Alamy 19b William Lovelace/Getty 20 John Dominis/ Getty 23t Blank Archives/Getty 23c Blank Archives/Getty 23b Three Lions/Stringer/Getty 24t John Dominis/Getty 24b MediaPunch Inc/Alamy 25t United Archives GmbH/Alamy 26 Robert Noyes/Alamy 27–9 Ian Tyas/Stringer/Getty 30 Glastonbury Festivals 32t Ian Gavan/Getty 32b Felix Kunze/ Redferns/Getty 33t Joanne Newman/Alamy 33b Leon Neal/AFP/ Getty Images 34–5 Avalon/PYMCA/Gonzales Photo/Peter Troest/Universal Images Group/Getty Images 37t Jesper Bjarke Andersen 37c Flemming Bo Jensen 37b Vegard S. Kristiansen 38 Trinity Mirror/Mirrorpix/Alamy 40t Reading and Leeds Festival/ Festival Republic 40b Nicky J. Sims/Redferns/Getty 41t PYMCA/ Universal Images Group/Getty Images 41c Gary Wolstenholme/ Redferns/Getty 41b Stuart Mostyn/Redferns/Getty 42 Heritage Image Partnership Ltd/Alamy 44 Steve Speller/Alamy 47t Tricia de Courcy Ling/Alamy 47c Patricia Phillips/Stockimo/Alamy 47b Samir Hussein/Getty 48 Agencja Fotograficzna Caro/Alamy 49 The Genesis Archive 50 Gina Wetzler/Getty 51 dpa picture alliance/Alamy 52 Dave Hogan/Hulton Archive/Getty 54 Bob Wick/BLM/Alamy 57 BLM Photo/Alamy 58t lukas bischoff/Alamy 58b BLM Photo/Alamy 59t Scott London/Alamy 59b BLM Photo/ Alamy 60 MICHAEL KAPPELER/DDP/AFP/Getty 63t Günther/ ullstein bild/Getty 63c MICHAEL KAPPELER/DDP/AFP/Getty 63b Andreas Rentz/Getty 64 Ebet Roberts/Redferns/Getty 65 Lane Turner/The Boston Globe/Getty 67 Michael Hickey/Getty 68 Cavan Images/Alamy 70 Paul Hennessy/NurPhoto/Getty 71t Paul Hennessy/Alamy 71c Everett Collection Inc/Alamy 71b Paul Hennessy/Alamy 72 Oleg Nikishin/Getty 73 Benoit Gysembergh/ Paris Match/Getty 74 Antoine GYORI/Sygma/Getty 75 Benoit Gysembergh/Paris Match/Getty 76 Andrew Meares/The Sydney Morning Herald/Fairfax Media/Getty 77 Mark Metcalfe/Getty 78t ABC 78b nzhistory.govt.nz 79t Fairfax Media/Getty 79b Andrew Meares/Fairfax Media/Getty 80 Sandor Csudai 81 citizeninsane. eu 82t Sandor Csudai 82c Zoltan Csipke/Alamy 82b Sandor Csudai 84 Xavi Torrent/WireImage/Getty 86 The Asahi Shimbun/Getty 88 Fuji Rock Festival 89 Kiyoshi Ota/Getty 90 SGranitz/WireImage/Getty 92 classicposters.com 93t SGranitz/ WireImage/Getty 93c CHERYL MEYER/Star Tribune/Getty 93b CHERYL MEYER/Star Tribune/Getty 94 Janis Trausch 96 Catherina Stuckmann 97t Lea GK 97c Christian Hedel 97b Nicola Rehbein 98 Tuska Festival 100t Tuska Festival 100b Aija Lehtonen/Shutterstock 101 Aija Lehtonen/Shutterstock 102 Martyn Goodacre/Getty 104 PYMCA/Universal Images Group/ Getty 106 ARCTIC IMAGES/Alamy 107t Florian Trykowski www. nordicmusic.photography 107c Ásgeir Helgi 107b Mathias Rhode/ Alamy 108 Presley Ann/Getty 109 DAVID MCNEW/AFP/Getty 111 Emma McIntyre/Getty 112t Kevin Mazur/Getty 112b John Sciulli/ Getty 113t VALERIE MACON/AFP/Getty 113b Scott Dudelson/ Getty 114 Zak Kaczmarek/Getty 116–7 Mark Metcalfe/Getty 118

Xavi Torrent/WireImage/Getty 119 Raphael Dias/Redferns/Getty 120 Primavera Sound 121t Miguel Pereira/Alamy 121c Design Pics Inc/Alamy 121b Miguel Pereira/WireImage/Getty 122 Paul Perton – AfricaRising/Alamy 124 Tyson Jopson/Shutterstock 125t Xinhua/Alamy 125c Xinhua/Alamy 125b Paul Perton – AfricaRising/Alamy 126 Andrew Aitchison/Alamy 128 Lovebox 129t Andrew Aitchison/Alamy 129c Matt Kent/WireImage/Getty 129b Simone Joyner/Getty 130 JEAN-PHILIPPE KSIAZEK/AFP/ Getty 132–5 Bang Face Weekender 136 Christian Bertrand/ Alamy 138 Joseph Okpako/WireImage/Getty 140–1 WENN Rights Ltd/Alamy 142–3 Download Festival 144 roger parkes/Alamy 147t roger parkes/Alamy 147c roger parkes/Alamy 147b Patricia Phillips/Stockimo/Alamy 148 Ollie Millington/WireImage/Getty 149 Joseph Okpako/WireImage/Getty 151t Ollie Millington/ WireImage/Getty 151c Ollie Millington/WireImage/Getty 151b Joseph Okpako/WireImage/Getty 152 Petri Anttila 153–4 Konstantin Kondrukhov 155t Petri Anttila 155c Konstantin Kondrukhov 155b Petri Anttila 156 steve mcinerny/Alamy 157 Jean Jameson 158 Lake of Stars 159t Jean Jameson 159c Steve McInerny 159b Steve McInerny 160 Cynthia Edorh/Getty 162 Roger Kisby/Getty 163 Kris Connor/Getty 164t Paras Griffin/ Getty 164b Jason Mendez/Getty 165t Paras Griffin/Getty 165b Paras Griffin/Getty 166 Ilan Deutsch/Paris Match/Getty 167 DAVID PINTENS/AFP/Getty 169t DAVID PINTENS/AFP/Getty 169c Ilan Deutsch/Paris Match/Getty 169b JONAS ROOSENS/ AFP/Getty 170 Rune Hellestad - Corbis/Corbis/Getty 172 Way Out West 173t Rune Hellestad - Corbis/Corbis/Getty 173c Ragnar Singsaas/WireImage/Getty 173b Ragnar Singsaas/ WireImage/Getty 174–7 courtesy of Movement Entertainment 178–181 Jackie Dixon 182 Dan Medhurst 184 Bart Heemskerk 186–7 Ian Duncan Kacungira 188 Bwette Photography 189t Bwette Photography 189b IAN DUNCAN KACUNGIRA/AFP/Getty 190 Tim Buiting 192–5 REBECCA CONWAY/AFP/Getty 196 SOLOVOV.be 197 Liam Simmons 198 Josh Hiatt for Here & Now 199–200 SOLOVOV.be 201 Josh Hiatt for Here & Now 202t Josh Hiatt for Here & Now 202b AJR Photos 203t Josh Hiatt for Here & Now 203b SOLOVOV.be 204 Luke Dyson 206–7 WENN Rights Ltd/Alamy 208–9t Luke Dyson 209b Garry Jones Photography 210 Ricardo Rubio/Europa Press/Getty 211 Mariano Regidor/ Redferns/Getty 212 Juan Aguado/Redferns/Getty 213 Mariano Regidor/Redferns/Getty 214–5 Sandor Csudai